BE YOUR OWN DOCTOR WITH

FOOT REFLEXOLOGY

By

Dr. Dhiren Gala
B.Sc., D.H.M.S., D.O., D.Ac.,
C.G.O., C.C.H., A.R.S.H.
Recipient of a gold medal for extraordinary
work in the field of Alternative Therapeutics

With

Dr. D. R. Gala
N.D., D.N.O., D.C.O.

Dr. Sanjay Gala
M.B. (BOM.), M.S. (ENT)

Knowledge is wealth

years of 1959 2009 imparting knowledge

NAVNEET PUBLICATIONS (INDIA) LIMITED

Navneet House
Gurukul Road, Memnagar,
Ahmadabad – 380 052.
Phone : 6630 5000

Navneet Bhavan
Bhavani Shankar Road,
Dadar, Mumbai – 400 028.
Phone : 6662 6565

DHANLAL BROTHERS DISTRIBUTORS
70, Princess Street, Mumbai – 400 002.
Phone : 2201 7027/2205 3716

G 4519

Visit us at : www.navneet.com | **e-mail :** npil@navneet.com

Price : Rs. 60.00

Dr. Dhiren Gala

1st floor, Abbas Bldg. 'A',

Near Tilak Market, Jalbhai Lane,

Harkishandas Hospital Road,

Grant Road (East), Mumbai – 400 004.

Phone : 2386 7275

Time : 4.00 to 7.00 pm

FOREWORD

Dr. Dhiren Gala is a celebrated practitioner. Neither he nor his writings need any introduction to the medical profession. He has received the highest accolades from the Open International University for Complementary Medicines, Sri Lanka.

Like acupuncture and acupressure, reflexology is a therapeutic science of stimulating specific regions [on the soles] which have a correspondence with the internal organs and other structures of the body. Acupuncture and reflexology cause their healing effects by stimulating the flow of 'Qi' energy.

How reflexology works, is an enigma. The same question is just as complex to answer when applied to widely used therapies like aspirin or anaesthesia. Acupuncture and reflexology are also, therefore, used on a similar empirical basis as they are safe, simple, effective and economical.

I have had the privilege of perusing this excellent text. Dr. Dhiren Gala has presented the quintessence of **Foot Reflexology** in a simple language and in a clinically useful form. This classic is certainly a milestone in the Complementary Medicines. This publication will serve as a veritable guide to the student and the practitioner, no less to the initiated layperson.

(Lord Pandit Prof. Dr. Sir Anton Jayasuriya)
M.B.B.S. (Cey.), B.Sc. (Tor.), D. Phys. Med.,
R.C.P. (Lon.) & R.C.S. (Eng.), M.Ac.F. (Sri Lanka),
D.Sc. (Cum Laude) Wellington University,
M.F. Hom. M.A., F.Ac.F (India), Ph.D., D.Litt. (Honoris Causa)
Chairman, Medicina Alternativa International.
Dean, The Open International University for Complimentary Medicines.

NAVNEET PUBLICATIONS (INDIA) LIMITED

Mumbai : 1. Bhavani Shankar Road, Dadar, **Mumbai – 400 028.** (Tel. 6662 6565 • Fax : 6662 6470)
2. **Navyug Distributors :** Road No. 8, M. I. D. C., Next to Indian Institute of Packaging, Marol, Andheri (East), **Mumbai – 400 093.** (Tel. 2821 4186 • Fax : 2835 2758)

Ahmadabad : Navneet House, Gurukul Road, Memnagar, **Ahmadabad – 380 052.** (Tel. 6630 5000)

Bengalooru : Sri Balaji's, No. 12, 2nd Floor, 3rd Cross, Malleswaram, **Bengalooru – 560 003.** (Tel. 2346 5740)

Chennai : 30, Sriram Nagar, North Street, Alwarpet, **Chennai – 600 018.** (Tel. 2434 6404)

Delhi : 2-E/23, Orion Plaza, 2nd & 3rd Floor, Jhandewalan Extn., **New Delhi – 110 055.** (Tel. 2361 0170)

Hyderabad : Kalki Plaza, Plot No. 67, Krishnapuri Colony, West Maredpalley, **Secunderabad – 500 026.** (Tel. 2780 0146)

Kolkata : 1st Floor, 7, Suren Tagore Road, **Kolkata – 700 019.** (Tel. 2460 4178)

Nagpur : 63, Opp. Shivaji Science College, Congress Nagar, **Nagpur – 440 012.** (Tel. 242 1522)

Nashik : Dharmaraj Plaza, Old Gangapur Naka, Gangapur Road, **Nashik – 422 005.** (Tel. 231 0627)

Navsari : 3/C, Arvind Nagar Society, Lunsikui Road, **Navsari – 396 445.** (Tel. 244 186)

Patna : 205, Jagdamba Tower, 2nd Floor, Sahdeo Mahto Marg, Srikrishnapuri, **Patna – 800 001.** (Tel. 254 0321)

Pune : Navneet Bhavan, 1302, Shukrawar Peth, Near Sanas Plaza, Bajirao Road, **Pune – 411 002.** (Tel. 2443 1007)

Rajkot : 20-21, Jagnath Corner, B/h Dhanrajani Building, Yagnik Road, **Rajkot – 360 001.**

Surat : 1, Ground Floor, Sri Vallabh Complex, Kotwal Street, Nanpara, **Surat – 395 001.** (Tel. 246 3927)

Vadodara : Near Hanuman Wadi, Sardar Bhuvan Khancho, **Vadodara – 390 001.**

Published by Navneet Publications (India) Ltd., Dantali, Gujarat.
Printed by Trishla Offset, Ahmedabad – 81.

[19 – 1 – 2009 (11) : 3]

PREFACE

Of late, a lot of public interest has been aroused in **Reflex Zone Therapy (Reflexology).** Disillusioned with medicines, more and more people are looking for alternative modes of treatment. To satisfy their curiosity and to meet their needs, a number of books on Reflexology have sprung up.

As we read some of these books we realize and, therefore, feel concerned about the fact that somewhere along the way, this therapy has become contaminated with mistruths and unreasonable claims of efficacy. Many of these books are chatty, repetitive, sometimes confusing and usually chock-full of unproved statements and facile explanations. And a few books even venture to prescribe Ayurvedic, Biochemic and Homoeopathic medicines. Come to think of it : A book on Reflexology suggesting medicinal treatment to people who are tired of medicines.

Naturally, such books tend to antagonize scientifically trained minds. It is for this reason that Reflexology has not found favour with qualified doctors. Thus, its development and advancement have been hindered.

We, therefore, feel that the time has come to establish the basic tenets of Reflex Zone Therapy. We realize that a book should be brought out which (1) presents scientific facts about Reflexology in clear, simple language and (2) brings together and collates all diverse information involving treatment on key points of the feet.

We have sought to bring all pertinent material up-to-date and to discuss it in an intelligible manner. Moreover, for the sake of objectivity and going against common practice, we have refrained from cluttering the book with personal anecdotes and numerous accounts of miraculous case histories, that do nothing but impose pressure upon the credibility of the reader.

This is truly a 'do-it-yourself' book. There is nothing complex or difficult about the techniques described. They are well within the reach of any person, even the most untrained or the one without any previous medical knowledge.

Though the scope of Reflexology is wide and its efficacy remarkable, **we do not claim that the pressure treatment suggested here will work in each and every case in spite of the most conscientious applications.** Indeed, no therapy (not even a medical science) can boast of cent per cent success. If a condition does not improve even after a considerably long course of treatment, or seems to be getting worse, the reader should consult his physician.

–Authors

CONTENTS

PART I : INTRODUCTION

PART II : REFLEX ZONE THERAPY

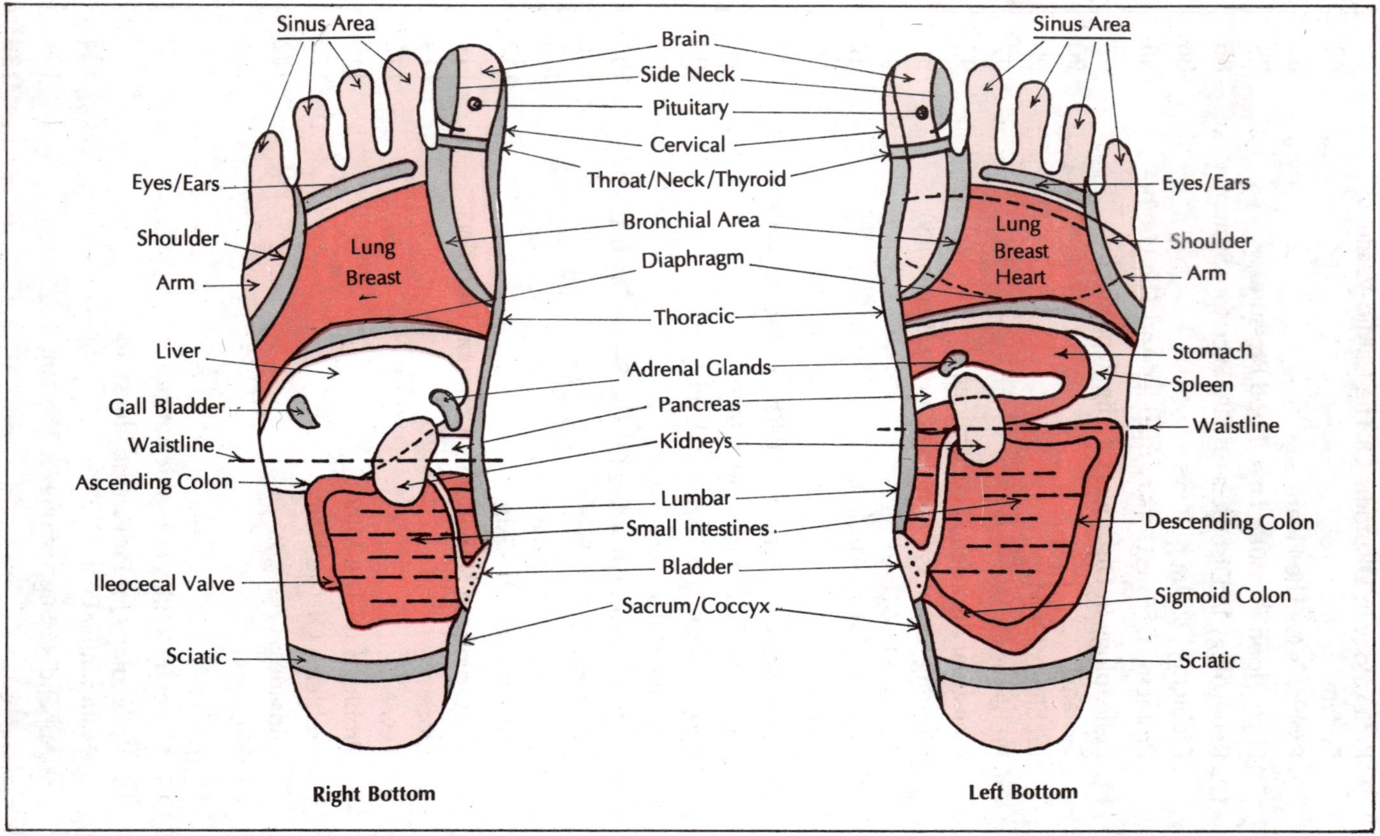
Sinus Area
Eyes/Ears
Shoulder
Arm
Lung
Breast
Liver
Gall Bladder
Waistline
Ascending Colon
Ileocecal Valve
Sciatic
Right Bottom
Brain
Side Neck
Pituitary
Cervical
Throat/Neck/Thyroid
Bronchial Area
Diaphragm
Thoracic
Adrenal Glands
Pancreas
Kidneys
Lumbar
Small Intestines
Bladder
Sacrum/Coccyx
Sinus Area
Eyes/Ears
Lung
Breast
Heart
Shoulder
Arm
Stomach
Spleen
Waistline
Descending Colon
Sigmoid Colon
Sciatic
Left Bottom

PART I

1. INTRODUCTION

Reflex Zone Therapy or simply Reflexology is a non-medicinal form of treatment in which specific spots on the surface of the body, usually the soles or the palms, are methodically pressed with a view to suitably influencing the internal organs of the body. Alternatively, Reflexology can be defined as a science of stimulating points (usually on the soles or the palms) which have a correspondence or a link with internal organs of the body.

Like Acupuncture or Acupressure, even Reflexology has its roots in antiquity. A form of treatment by means of pressure points was prevalent in India and China almost 5000 years ago. A similar form of therapy was practised in ancient Egypt too. A picture (reproduced below) found on the tomb of Ankhmahar (king's physician) at Saqquara in Egypt clearly shows 'Reflexology' being 'practised'. Studies have shown this tomb to be about 4500 years old.

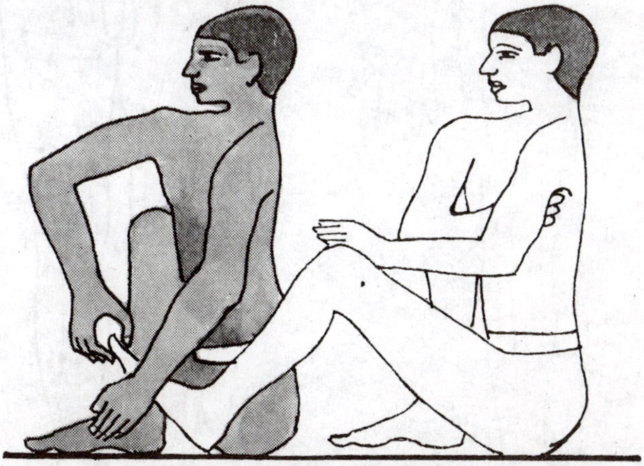

Fig. 1.1 : Reflexology in ancient Egypt

It can be presumed that Acupuncture and Reflexology originated from a common root. There are a number of things common to Acupuncture and Reflexology. Both recognize a flow, in the body, of energy (bio-electricity). In Reflexology, this flow is thought to take place through zones whereas in Acupuncture the flow is thought to occur through 'meridians'. In both these therapies, one aim of treatment is to render this flow of energy smooth and harmonious.

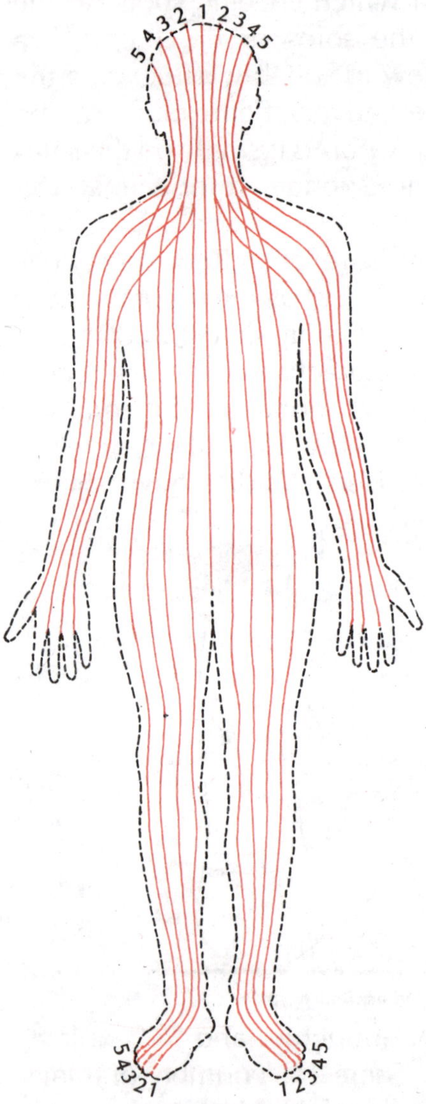

Fig. 1.2 : Reflex Zones

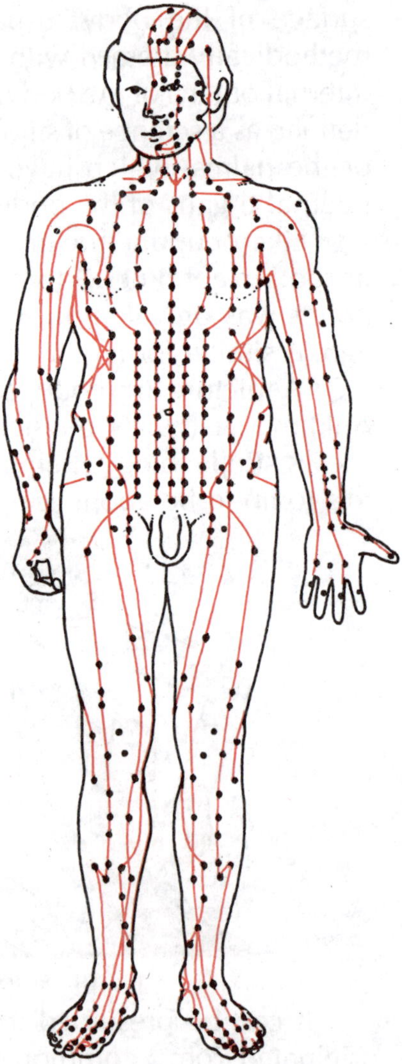

Fig. 1.3 : Acu Meridians

Due to reasons unknown, the shoot of Acupuncture flourished whereas that of Reflexology withered. However, it did not perish completely because it had become ingrained in some cultures. Indian, Chinese and North American tribals continued to employ it.

The great Florentine sculptor, Cellini (1500–1571 A.D.) exerted strong pressure on his toes and fingers to relieve pain anywhere in the body with remarkable success.

In central European countries similar methods were described by Dr. Adamus and Dr. A'Tatis in 1582 A.D. At about the same time, Dr. Ball of Leipzig (Germany) published a booklet describing treatment of organs through pressure points. The twentieth American president W. Garfield (1831-1881 A.D.) was able to alleviate the pains he had, following an assassination attempt on his life, by applying pressure to various points in his feet. Pain-killing medicines could give him no relief.

Another exponent of pressure therapy was Dr. H. Bressler. Dr. Bressler's work and success generated a lot of interest in Dr. William Fitzgerald (1872–1942 A.D.). Dr. Fitzgerald graduated in medicine from the University of Vermount in 1895. For two years he was on the staff of Central London Ears, Nose and Throat Hospital. Later, he started practising as a physician at the Boston City Hospital and as a laryngologist at St. Francis ENT Hospital in Hartford, Connecticut. It was in 1902 A.D., while he was the head of ENT department that he was drawn to pressure therapy. He started working on toes and fingers of his patients to quickly realize that this produced considerable analgesia and relieved headaches, earaches, tummy-aches, etc.

While other doctors like H. Bressler had employed pressure therapy infrequently on a few patients, Dr. Fitzgerald started to employ it methodically on most of the patients who came to him. He achieved great success in his endeavours. He took great pains to make this therapy known to doctors. Therefore, Dr. Fitzgerald can be considered the rediscoverer of Reflexology. He gave it a fresh lease of life.

Dr. Fitzgerald evolved a theory that divided the human body longitudinally into five zones on the left and five zones on the right. He had realized that any problem of an organ lying in one particular zone could be treated by applying pressure somewhere else within the same zone.

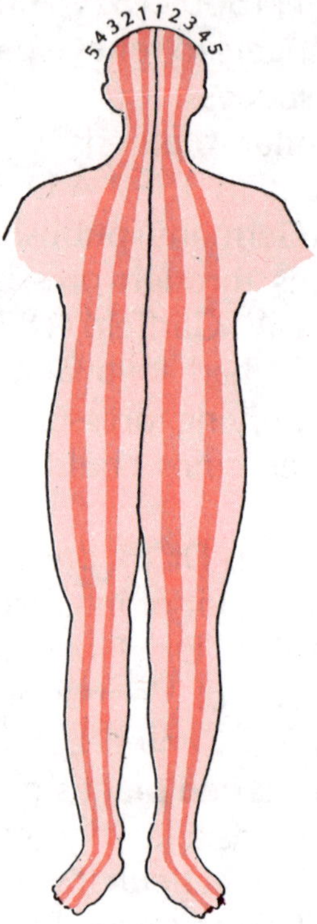

Fig. 1.4 : Fitzgerald's ten vertical zones

Zone therapy was further popularized by Dr. Edwin Bowers M.D., an early associate of Dr. Fitzgerald. He developed a unique and startling method for convincing his colleagues about the validity of zone theory. He would apply pressure to a colleague's hand and then stick a pin in the corresponding area (zone) of his face anaesthesized by the pressure. Such dramatic proof made believers out of those who witnessed it. Along with Dr. Fitzgerald, Dr. Bowers brought out the first book on pressure therapy entitled 'Zone Therapy'. It contained therapeutic recommendations and guidelines for doctors, dentists, gynaecologists, ENT specialists and others.

Reflex Zone Therapy was given further impetus by Dr. George White and Dr. Joseph Riley.

Working in Dr. Riley's office was a therapist, Eunice Ingham. She had seen Dr. Riley working on patients' hands. If pressing on hands can influence internal organs, pressing on soles should also produce similar effects, she thought. Driven with this idea, she began probing the feet of all persons she came across, finding a tender spot and corelating it with the diseased internal organ. Such careful study enabled her to map the entire human body on the soles of the two feet. Dr. Fitzgerald divided each foot into five longitudinal zones; Eunice Ingham further subdivided it (with help of three lines) into four transverse zones.

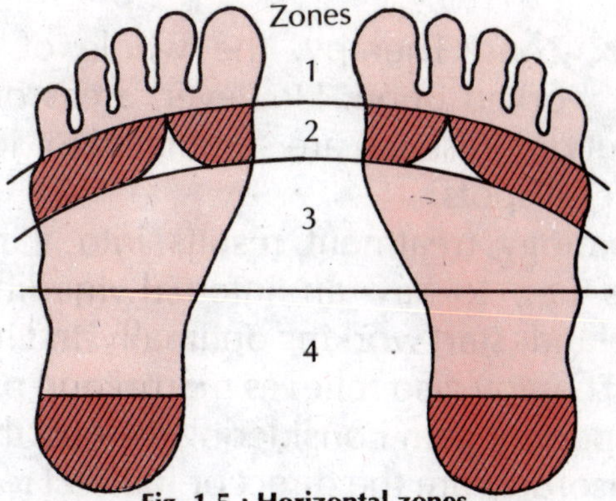

Fig. 1.5 : Horizontal zones

Eunice Ingham brought out two books 'Stories the feet can tell' and 'Stories the feet have told' describing her experiments and experiences with Foot Reflexology. She worked tirelessly to popularize Reflexology throughout the length and breadth of the U.S.A. It would not be an exaggeration to say that she put Foot Reflexology 'on its feet'.

From America, Reflexology soon spread to other countries including India. Thanks to dedicated efforts by members of such charitable institutions like Jai Bhagwan Acupressure Service, Bombay, All India Centre for Acupressure Research, Bombay, Indian Academy of Acupressure Science, Indore, etc., Reflexology has become extremely popular in India. These institutions have taken up the work of Reflexology with a missionary zeal.

In India, both Foot Reflexology and Hand Reflexology are equally popular. Foot Reflexology, however, enjoys certain advantages over Hand Reflexology. It is much easier to locate the trigger points for various organs on the feet than on the hands. This is because of the fact that a foot has a much bigger surface area than a hand and, therefore, gives a greater (bigger) representation to each organ. On the other hand, the trigger areas for various organs are compressed on the hand, rendering their location relatively difficult. Moreover, the trigger spots are situated somewhat deep on the hands. Therefore, a greater force (deeper pressure) is required to reach them. This entails much hard work and, therefore, may prove tiresome.

In Reflex Zone Therapy, the whole of each foot is methodically worked upon. However, areas or spots found tender (painful on pressure) are stimulated for longer periods than non-painful spots.

A Reflexology treatment results into a restoration of homoeostasis i.e., to say an internal equilibrium results. Organs and glands start working optimally and harmoniously. Reflex Zone Therapy also relieves mental and physical stress. This is an important gain considering the fact that in modern times most disorders are the direct or indirect results of stress. Reflexology stimulates the body's immune system i.e., it strengthens the body's natural resistance. Its resistance thus strengthened, the body can prevent or drive away any disease. Therefore, the scope of this therapy is virtually unlimited. It can be employed in the treatment of any disease that has not been rendered incurable by gross and irreversible pathological changes.

Reflexology is especially suitable for the treatment of the following disorders (the list is by no means exhaustive) :

Anorexia (loss of appetite), arthritis, backache, bedwetting in children, colds, constipation, cough, diarrhoea (loose motions), dizziness, ear disorders, eye disorders, flatulence (gas), giddiness, goitre, headache, hyperacidity, indigestion, insomnia, loss of voice, menstrual disorders, mental tension, migraine, nose disorders, painful disorders, painful joints, sinusitis, sore throat, thyroid disorders, tonsillitis, toothache.

Reflexology should also be tried (and frequently gives good results) in disorders with vague symptoms like 'a feeling of malaise', general lassitude, chronic fatigue, pain in bones, trembling of the body, etc. Here, due to difficulty in arriving at a diagnosis, rational medicinal treatment is impossible to administer.

Moreover, Reflexology should form an essential part of treatment of all such diseases which have no satisfactory medical solution or which are considered incurable and, therefore, require to be treated throughout life. Such diseases include high blood pressure, diabetes mallitus, asthma, rheumatoid arthritis, osteo-arthritis, atherosclerosis, disseminated sclerosis, emphysema, jaundice, systemic lupus erythematosus, etc.

However, among all therapeutic sciences, there is not one form of therapy which does not have its limitations. Indeed, not even medical science can claim to cure each and every case that comes to its attention. And Reflexology is no exception. In the following diseases, Reflexology should not be employed as the sole form of treatment; it can only be employed in conjunction with medicines :

All fulminating infections, pneumonia, tuberculosis, leprosy, serious disorders of the heart, kidney failure, meningitis, tumours, cancer etc.

Finally, Reflexology has no role to play in such purely mechanical disorders like congenital anomalies (viz. cleft palate, heart valvular defects), mature cataract, varicosed veins, hernia, big stones in gall bladder/urinary tract, prolapsed uterus, prolapsed rectum, a foreign body in eye/ear/nose, fracture, big abscesses, etc.

Similarly, Reflexology cannot help disorders arising from deficiencies of essential nutrients like proteins, vitamins and minerals.

In conclusion, it can be said that Reflex Zone Therapy is a non-medicinal, natural form of treatment that is extremely popular in all nooks and corners of the world. It is a boon to mankind because–

(a) It is extremely simple; even a small child can learn it. Therefore, it can be used as self-treatment.

(b) It is amazingly effective, sometimes producing almost miraculous results.

(c) It is absolutely safe unlike medicines (which produce untoward side effects).

(d) It is inexpensive since no medicines are required and you need not rush to a doctor for trivial ailments.

(e) It can be used alone or in conjunction with conventional medicines.

(f) It can be used to preserve peak health, prevent diseases and slow down ageing process.

However, the reader should understand that Reflexology is no panacea. It is not a 'cure all' and should not be considered an alternative to competent medical care. It is, in fact, a means of enabling the body to attain a perfect balance in all its functions. It arouses and activates the natural healing forces that have been suppressed and, therefore, rendered ineffective by disease-forces.

2. THE ZONE THEORY

Zone theory is the basis of Reflexology. Zones are a system for formulating relationships between various parts of the body. They can be thought of as guidelines or markers which link one part of the body to another.

There are ten equal longitudinal (vertical) zones running the length of the body from the top of the head to the tips of toes. (See Fig. 2.1.)

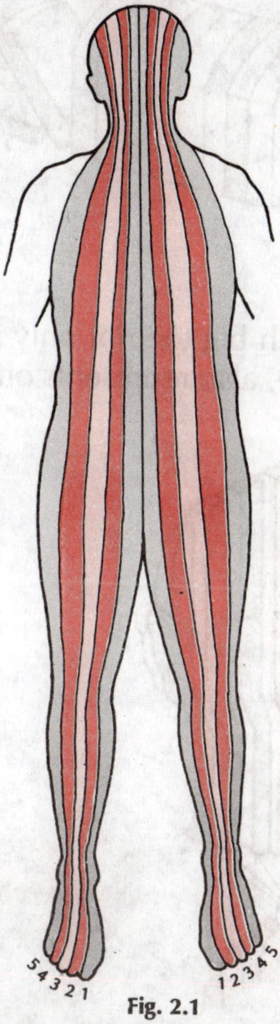

Fig. 2.1

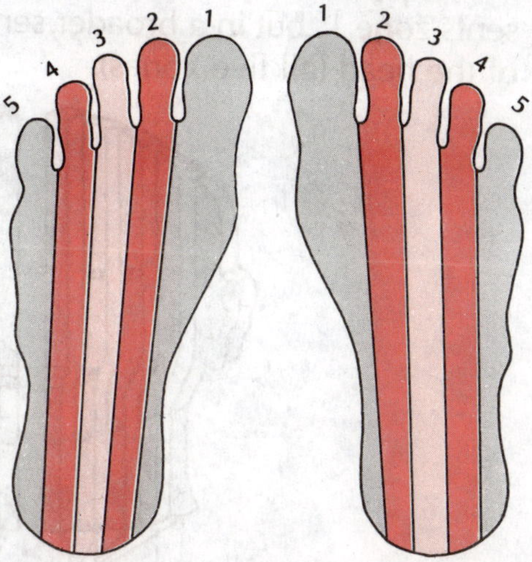

Fig. 2.2

On soles, the zones would look as shown in Fig. 2.2 above. Thus, each toe is a part of one particular zone.

It should be noted that a zone is not a surface marking. In fact, it runs through and through the body much like an arrow piercing from the front and emerging from the back. In other words, zones can be compared to slices of bread.

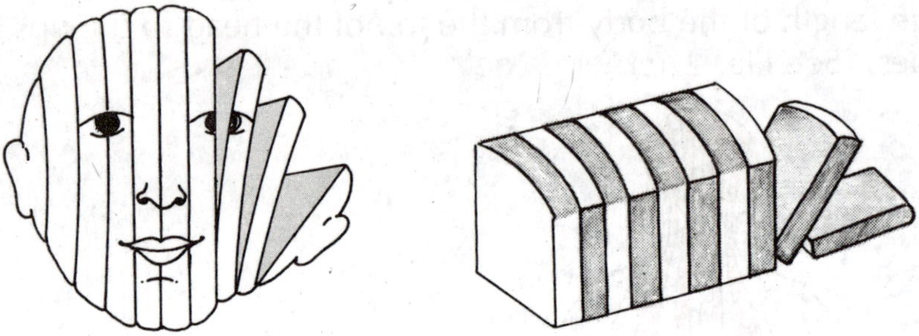

Fig. 2.3

Experience has shown that each big toe not only represents zone 1, but in a broader sense, also represents one half of the head (all five zones).

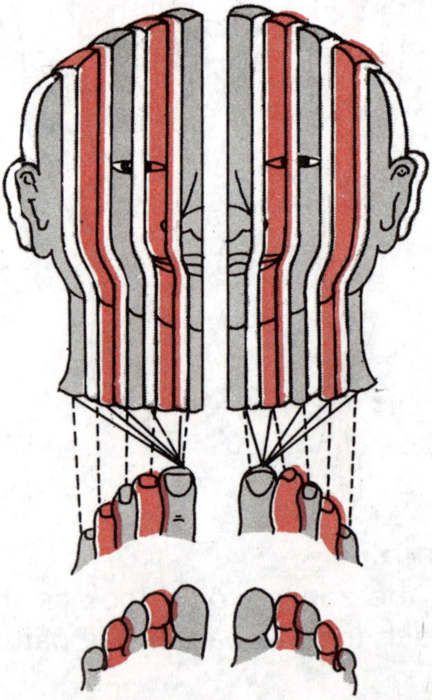

Fig. 2.4 : The big toe represents all five zones of the head

Dr. Fitzgerald propounded the theory that anything wrong in any part of a zone will affect the entire zone running through the whole length of the body. Sensitivity (tenderness or pain) in a specific spot on the foot points to the fact that something is wrong somewhere in the zone(s) in which the tender spot lies.

While Dr. Fitzgerald believed that a particular organ or a part of the body could be completely influenced through a toe (or toes) corresponding to the same zone(s), later experiments revealed that stimulation merely of toes did not always serve the purpose adequately. For a more certain treatment of various organs, specific parts of foot, along the entire soles, called for stimulation. This gave rise to the concept of lateral (horizontal) zones.

The main purpose of lateral zones is to help fix the image of the body onto the feet in the proper perspective and location. The lateral zones have been shown below.

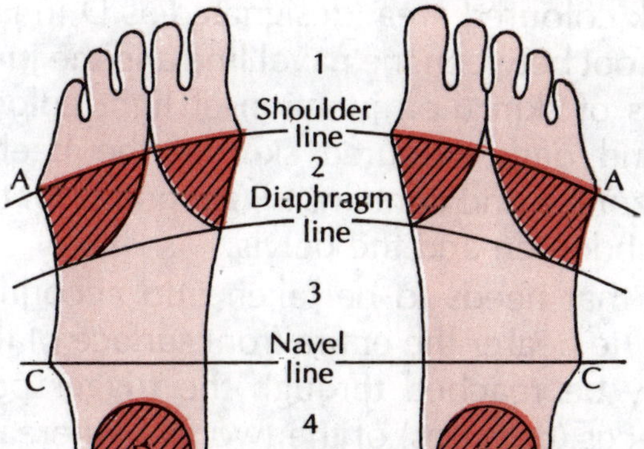

Fig. 2.5

On the fore-foot, at the sides you will find two prominent bones (designated as A and B in Fig. 2.5). On your sole, draw a transverse line passing through the tips of these prominent bones. This line is the shoulder line. The area of the foot from toe-tips to this shoulder line comprises horizontal zone 1 and contains trigger points for the organs of the head and neck.

If you observe the sole of the fore-foot, you will find two mountain-like structures. These are called the 'balls' of the foot. These balls are of a much darker colour as compared to the middle of the sole. On your sole, draw a line passing through the lower borders of the balls. This is the diaphragm line. Diaphragm is a dome-shaped muscle that separates the chest from the abdomen. The area of the foot between the shoulder line and the diaphragm line comprises horizontal zone 2 and contains trigger points for organs of the chest.

Almost at the middle of the outer border of the foot is another prominent bone (designated as C in Fig. 2.5). On your sole, draw a transverse line passing through this prominent bone. This line is the navel or waist line. In anatomical terminology, this line represents the 'L_4 (the fourth lumbar vertebra)' level. The area of the foot between the diaphragm and the navel lines comprises horizontal zone 3 and contains trigger points for most organs of abdomen.

If you observe the sole of the heel, you will find an oblong dark coloured area (designated as D in Fig. 2.5). The area of the foot between the navel line and the junction of the two colours of skin (i.e., junction of light coloured skin of mid-sole and dark coloured skin of the heel) comprises horizontal zone 4 and contains trigger points for the organs of the lower abdomen and the pelvis.

A fact that needs to be taken into account is that the organs that lie nearer the entire front surface of the body can more easily be reached through the trigger points on the upper surfaces (dorsums) of the two feet whereas the organs that lie nearer the entire back surface of the body can more easily be reached through the trigger points on the soles.

With the help of these four horizontal zones and the ten vertical zones (five on each foot) described earlier, you can most accurately determine or locate the trigger area for any organ whose correct anatomical position (i.e., the actual position inside the human body) is known to you.

3. WHAT HAPPENS AFTER PRESSURE TREATMENT AND WHY ?

How does the body react to pressure treatment ? What changes occur inside the body following Reflex Zone Therapy ? Why do such changes take place ?

Of the above questions, the first two can be answered more or less completely. However, all answers to the third question are not yet known.

The reactions of the body to Reflex Zone Therapy can be classified into : (I) Local reactions and (II) General reactions. Let us, now, try to understand these reactions.

Local reactions are those which are produced on all organs that happen to lie in the same zone as the toe (or longitudinal section of foot) that is stimulated. Let us try to understand this with the help of the figure given below :

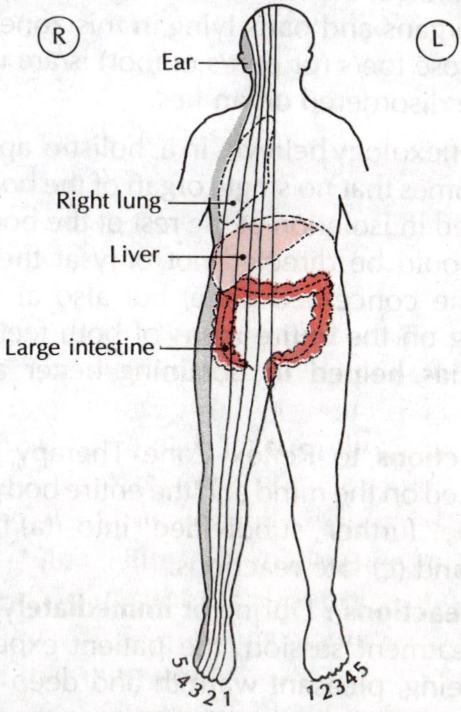

Fig. 3.1

You will recall that from the observed facts, Dr. Fitzgerald was led to suspect and later believe in the existence of ten longitudinal zones in the body. These zones have been shown in Fig. 3.1. If the little toe of the right foot is stimulated, all body-parts and organs lying in zone R_5 (viz. outer aspects of right foot-leg-thigh, right side of trunk, a part of large intestine, a part of liver, right side of neck, right molar teeth, right outer ear, right temple, etc.) are affected.

The exact nature of affection usually depends upon (1) the method and (2) the duration of stimulation. For example, alternating (press-release-press-release type of) stimulation of little toe for a short period will cause a mild stimulation of the various organs or parts of zone R_5. These organs have been enlisted in the previous paragraph. However, constant and prolonged stimulation of the same toe will gradually cause an analgesia of the organs and parts lying in this zone. Thus, in treatment, that/those toe/s (or part/s of foot) is/are utilized in whose zone/s the disordered organ lies.

However, Reflexology believes in a 'holistic' approach to treatment. It presumes that no single organ of the body can be healthy or diseased in isolation of the rest of the body. It says that treatment should be directed not only at the diseased organ (through the concerned zone) but also at the entire body (by working on the entire areas of both feet). Indeed, such approach has helped in obtaining better and faster results.

General reactions to Reflex Zone Therapy are those which are produced on the mind and the entire body. General reactions can be further subdivided into (a) immediate (b) intermediate and (c) late reactions.

Immediate reactions : During or **immediately** following a Reflexology treatment session, the patient experiences a feeling of well-being, pleasant warmth and deep relaxation (unless the treatment has been too vigorous, causing pain). Thanks to this release of tension, the person, many a time, falls asleep and awakens a short time later, much refreshed.

Intermediate reactions : Two or three days after the commencement of treatment, quite a few persons encounter one or more of the following reactions :

- an increase in the activity of the skin, with increased perspiration, which is sometimes malodorous.
- an increase in the urinary output.
- an increase in the bulk and, sometimes, frequency of stools.
- an increase in the secretions from the mucous membranes of nose, pharynx and bronchi, signifying a cleansing process.
- occasionally, a feeling of mild pain and general malaise in the body, with or without fever.

These are merely signs of a re-activation of body's defence forces that are trying to eliminate toxins and waste-materials accumulated in the body. These unpleasant reactions are purely temporary, do not permanently harm and, therefore, should cause no alarms.

With the body progressively getting free of toxins, the above mentioned reactions rapidly diminish in intensity and ultimately disappear.

It should be noted that such reactions do not necessarily affect each and every person. Indeed, many fortunate persons straight away start exhibiting the late or delayed reactions described below :

Delayed reactions commence after the body has been rendered reasonably free of toxins. These comprise a restoration of homoeostasis (i.e., a return of bodily functions like temperature, blood pressure, respiratory rate, heart-rate acid-base balance, etc., towards a state of normalcy or balance) and an increase in the body's immunity (natural resistance) marked by a rise in the number of white blood corpuscles and titre of gamma globulin.

With its toxins eliminated and its immunity strengthened, the body is able to drive away the disease.

The above are the effects of Reflex Zone Therapy. Let us now take up the question of how these effects are produced.

While Reflexology's actions are well-known, the precise mechanism of these actions has not yet been unravelled (discovered). A number of theories have been put forward by research scientists. The most popular and widely accepted among them is the nervous theory which claims that the effects produced on the diseased organ, following pressure treatment, are the results of cutaneo-visceral 'autonomic' reflex action.

Before elaborating upon this theory, let us obtain the answers to two basic questions : (1) What is a disease? and (2) What is a reflex action?

(1) Each and every organ, gland or part of our body shows some electrical activity. Electrical activity of the heart, the brain and a muscle can be measured or assessed by instruments like ECG (Electro-cardiogram), EEG (Electro-encephalogram) and EMG (Electro-myogram) respectively. In health, this electrical activity is maintained within a narrow range. If gross changes occur in the electrical activity of an organ, it contracts a disease. In other words, disease is nothing but an outcome of a disturbance in the electrical activity of an organ.

(2) A reflex action is the one that takes place without the intervention of the brain. For example, if you inadvertently touch something very hot, the hand is automatically (reflexly) withdrawn. Only afterwards do you realize that you had touched a hot object. Thus, action (withdrawal of the hand) occurs before the realization on the part of brain. Reflex actions are essentially protective in nature.

According to the supporters of the nervous theory, the action of pressure therapy on any particular organ is the result of a reflex due to which normal electrical activity is restored. In other words, restoration of health following pressure therapy is a reflex reaction of an organ to an electrical impulse produced by stimulation of specific spots on soles/palms/body.

A probable pathway of this reflex is as under :

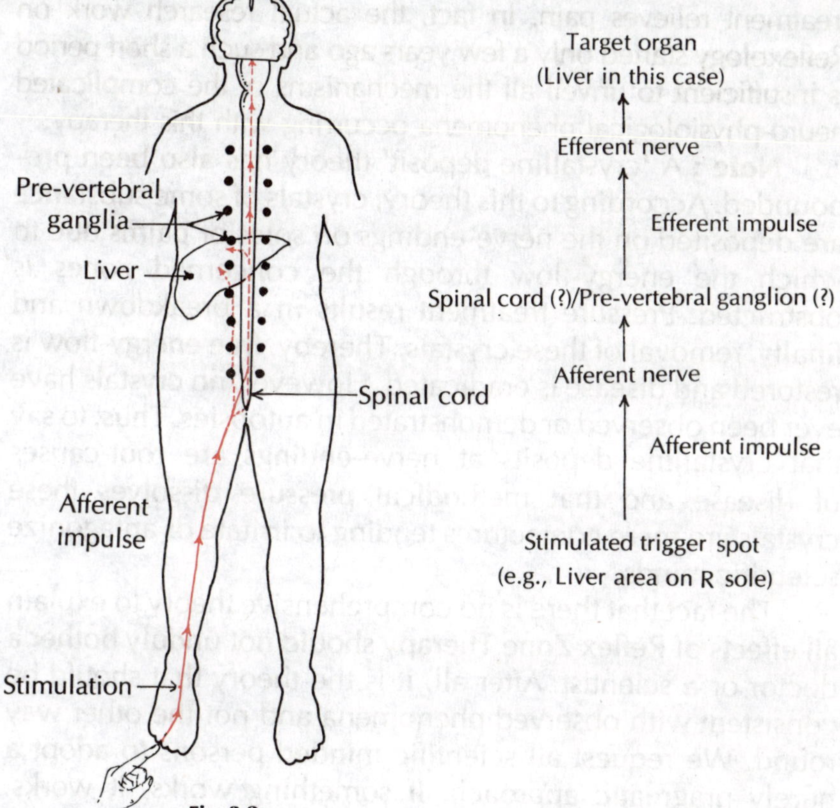

Fig. 3.2

Moreover, it is believed that a few of the impulses (generated by pressure) also manage to reach the hypothalamus, which is the seat of autonomous nervous system and the controller of sympatho-parasympathetic activity. The mutually opposing sympathetic and parasympathetic systems then get balanced, due to which homoeostasis is restored.

This 'nervous' theory to explain the mechanism of action of pressure therapy is quite convincing considering the fact that there are over 7200 nerve-endings in each foot. These have extensive interconnections, through the spinal cord and the brain, with all areas of the body.

However, this theory cannot explain all the effects of Reflex Zone Therapy. It fails to explain how prolonged pressure treatment relieves pain. In fact, the actual research work on Reflexology started only a few years ago and such a short period is insufficient to unveil all the mechanisms of the complicated neuro-physiological phenomena occurring with this therapy.

Note : A 'crystalline deposit' theory has also been propounded. According to this theory, crystals of some substance are deposited on the nerve-endings on soles or palms due to which the energy-flow through the concerned zones is obstructed. Pressure treatment results in a breakdown and finally, removal of these crystals. Thereby, free energy-flow is restored and disease is eradicated. However, no crystals have ever been observed or demonstrated in autopsies. Thus, to say that crystalline deposits at nerve-endings are root-causes of disease and that methodical pressure dissolves these crystals are mere conjectures tending to irritate or antagonize scientific minds.

The fact that there is no comprehensive theory to explain all effects of Reflex Zone Therapy should not unduly bother a doctor or a scientist. After all, it is the theory that should be consistent with observed phenomena and not the other way round. We request all scientific minded persons to adopt a purely pragmatic approach. If something works, it works, irrespective of whether we can scientifically explain it or not. Even before Isaac Newton discovered the 'law of gravity', every apple always fell to the ground (unless plucked from the tree by some creature)! If Reflexology alleviates human suffering, we suggest it should be practised, whether or not it can be fitted into the framework of established science. Some day, the actual reasons for the efficacy of Reflexology will be discovered and, then, they will make as much sense as any other scientific fact. In fact, we will go a step further and say that following research to determine the mechanism of action of Reflexology, secret facts about human physiology may emerge and these may revolutionize even modern theories of medicine!

4. ANSWERS TO SOME QUESTIONS PEOPLE COMMONLY ASK

Q. 1. How is Reflexology different from Acupressure?

Ans. In Foot Reflexology, the trigger points for various organs are thought to be located on the soles of the feet. In Acupressure, the trigger points are thought to be located on fourteen meridians on the body. In other words, in Reflexology, points to be stimulated are limited only to soles whereas in Acupressure, points to be stimulated are scattered all over the body.

Therefore, Reflexology is much simpler than Acupressure.

Q. 2. Some reflexologists (or acupressurists) resort to manipulations (pulls and pushes) on the back, neck, legs or arms. Are these parts of Reflexology?

Ans. Osteopaths, chiropractors and sometimes orthopaedic surgeons and physical therapists resort to manipulative treatment. However it has nothing to do with Reflexology or Acupressure.

Such pulls and pushes can be quite dangerous, and may turn out to be harmful, if received from an unqualified and/or inexperienced practitioner, especially if employed on the spine. Unless he is also an osteopath or a chiropractor, a reflexologist is not qualified to give manipulative treatment. So, do not mistake pulls, pushes and jerks for Reflexology.

Q. 3. While receiving Reflex Zone Therapy, should previous medicines be discontinued?

Ans. Some reflexologists do persuade their patients to give up medicines. However, Reflex Zone Therapy and medicinal therapy are not opposed to each other. Reflexology can be used in conjunction with medicines. We will say that neither start nor discontinue medicines unless instructed to do so by your physician.

Q. 4. Some doctors say that benefits of Reflexology are due to suggestion or faith. What do you say?

Ans. It is difficult to believe that suggestion or faith can produce such analgesia as would allow the Reflexologist to introduce pins in the treated person's body without causing any pain whatsoever.

Again, Reflexology benefits even children, insane persons and unconscious persons who are not amenable to suggestions.

Medical doctors who write off Reflexology saying its effects are merely results of suggestion should ponder over Dr. William Osler's words : "The history of medicine is the history of placebo!"

Q. 5. Is Reflexology safe even for babies, pregnant women and diabetics?

Ans. The most prominent effect of Reflex Zone Therapy is a restoration of equilibrium inside the body. There is no reason to believe that Reflexology will prove detrimental to the health of a baby, a pregnant woman or a diabetic. On the contrary, it has been seen that Reflexology (a) assists in normalizing or stimulating the growth of a child, (b) prevents or diminishes common problems of pregnancy (like nausea, vomiting, swelling on feet, high blood pressure, disorders of mood, etc.) and makes delivery easier and (c) helps a diabetic to keep blood sugar level under complete control.

Q. 6. Can Reflexology cause a heart attack?

Ans. The allegation that Reflexology may precipitate a heart attack is baseless. We will again reiterate that Reflex Zone Therapy works to normalize the functioning of internal organs and systems of the body. The cause of a heart attack is an obstruction of a blood vessel supplying the heart. A heart attack may be precipitated 'in spite' of receiving Reflex Zone Therapy but certainly not 'because' of it.

Q. 7. If Reflex Zones are present all over the body, why work only on the soles or palms?

Ans. Reflex zones are, indeed, present on the entire body. However, soles or palms are preferred for treatment because (a) they are quite thin (flattened) and, therefore, easy to work upon and (b) nerve-endings can be easily pressed against the underlying bones. Again, not many persons (especially women) will like the idea of other body-parts being worked upon.

Q. 8. Is Reflexology a sure method of diagnosis?

Ans. Presence (or absence) of pain at a particular spot on foot cannot be taken as an unfailing indication of presence (or absence) of disease in the corresponding organ. The symptoms of the patient, the clinical findings of the doctor and reports of investigations have to be co-related with the pain at a spot on a foot before diagnosis can be arrived at.

We will say that a reflexologist should not take upon himself the responsibility of diagnosing a disease. He should leave that job to a doctor.

Q. 9. If Reflexology is so effective, why is it not popular enough?

Ans. Reflexology is, indeed, a very simple and effective therapy. However, a lot of time needs to be devoted to stimulate various trigger points on the two feet. And time is one thing neither the people nor the doctors have. Moreover, Reflexology is considered just too much work. People have become easy-going. They find it easier to go by the apparently easy route : Let the doctor fix me up.

Finally, doctors have shown little interest in Reflexology. Even in medical profession, prejudice dies hard. Doctors, by and large, prefer to continue believing in their time-honoured methods rather than trying out something they have not learnt in a medical school.

Q. 10. Why don't all patients receiving Reflex Zone Therapy respond equally well?

Ans. Almost every person who receives Reflex Zone Therapy can benefit from it, but not all recover completely. Disregarding advice, some will continue to eat the wrong foods, drink the wrong beverages, refuse to give up tobacco, alcohol or narcotics and refuse to do away with that frown on their foreheads.

Again, if a patient's disease has progressed to an extent where irreversible pathological changes have taken place in his organs, he cannot be cured. Even if a disease is curable, not all persons suffering from that disease can be cured.

Q. 11. Many reflexologists advocate the use only of bare hands for treatment and strongly advise against using jimmies, rollers, rubber-bands, combs or clothes-pins. What do you say?

Ans. While treating a patient with hands (thumbs and fingers) is desirable, there should be no objection to an occasional use of gadgets enlisted above. Remember that the discoverer of Reflexology, Dr. Fitzgerald whole-heartedly recommended such gadgets. Then, why should his disciples discourage them?

Does a person with weak thumbs, arthritic fingers, inflexible ankles or fragile health, and desirous of treating himself, have any alternative but to resort to simple gadgets?

The campaign against gadgets is the result of some reflexologists' tendency to prevent people from shouldering the responsibility of treatment themselves. Indeed, such reflexologists have described complicated techniques and grip sequences to persuade people to believe that the treatment is quite complex and, therefore, beyond the reach of laymen. We say that the need of today is to demystify medicine.

Q. 12. Should a person receiving Reflex Zone Therapy follow certain rules about diet and exercise?

Ans. Reflex Zone Therapy does not allow a person to take liberties with his diet, or to lead a sedentary life.

Indeed, a well-balanced diet and regular exercise are indispensable for maintaining or regaining health.

Dietary restrictions/modifications are inevitable for the persons suffering from such disorders like colds, cough, constipation, piles, high B.P., diabetes, liver ailments, kidney ailments, heart ailments and obesity. A diabetic who continues to eat sweets cannot hope to improve with Reflex Zone Therapy.

---

5. PRACTICAL HINTS FOR TREATMENT

This chapter will tell you all about how to treat yourself (and your family members) through Reflexology successfully.

Before you start treating yourself or others, you should thoroughly prepare yourself, physically and mentally, for the purpose.

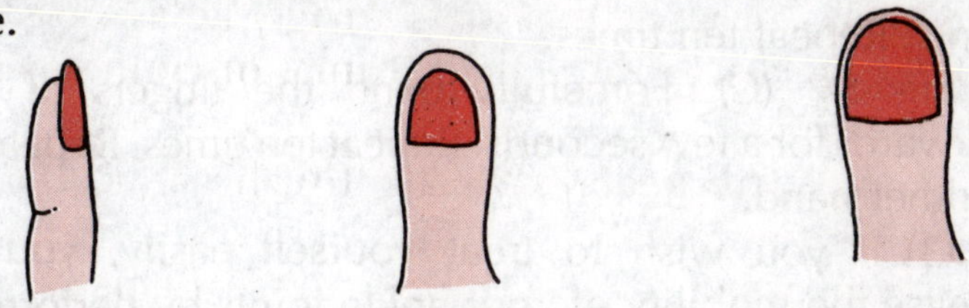

Nails should not be long. Nails should not be excessively clipped. Nails should be clipped proportionately.

Fig. 5.1

(1) Always keep your finger-nails well-trimmed with a nail-cutter and smoothened with a file. This will help you to avoid injury to the skin of the person you are treating. Moreover, pain produced by a sharp nail may be mistaken for 'real' tenderness of a spot on the sole/palm.

(2) Usually, Reflex Zone Therapy is given with the thumb or finger/s. Since a lot of pressure needs to be applied on the key spots of the sole, the thumb (or finger) soon tires and its joints start aching. This can, however, be avoided by performing some simple exercises to strengthen the hands. These have been depicted below :

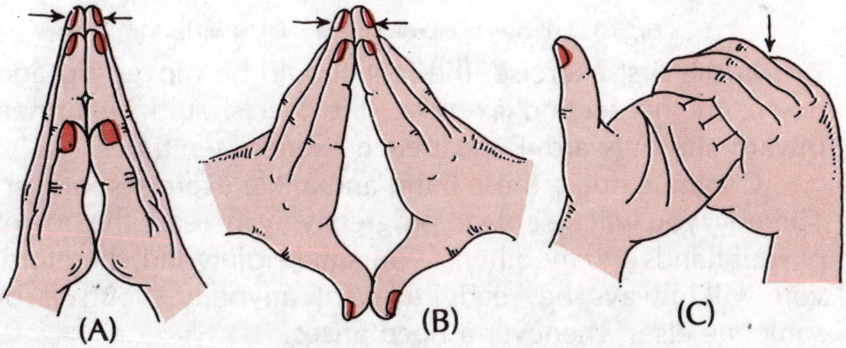

Fig. 5.2 : Exercises to strengthen the thumbs and the fingers

Fig. 5.2 (A) : Stand in 'Namaskara' pose. Firmly press the palms against each other for 10 counts. Repeat ten times.

Fig. 5.2 (B) : Keep the finger-tips and thumb-tips of the two hands in contact as shown. Exert pressure on the fingers and the thumb of one hand with those of the other for 10 counts. Repeat ten times.

Fig. 5.2 (C) : Forcefully bend the fingers of a hand backwards for a few seconds. Repeat ten times. Repeat this for the other hand.

(3) If you wish to treat yourself easily, you should increase the mobility of your ankle joints by performing the two simple exercises shown below :

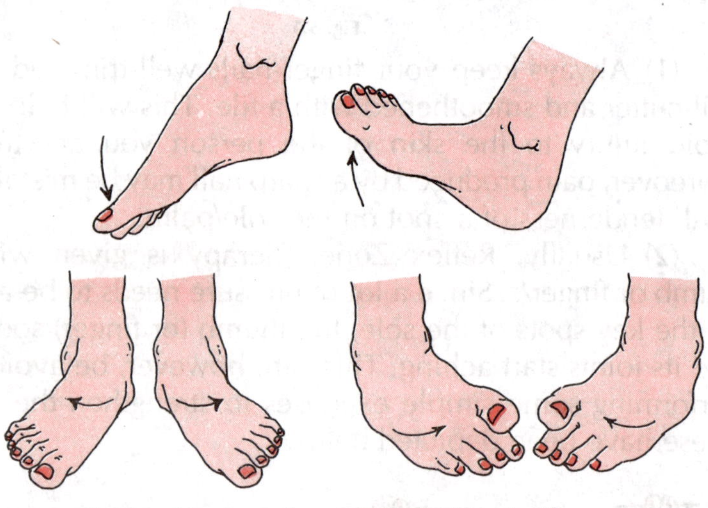

Fig. 5.3 : Exercises to increase the mobility of ankles

In the first exercise, the feet should be moved up and down. In the second exercise, the feet should be turned inward and outward. Repeat each exercise ten times.

Continue doing these hand and ankle exercises forever. Thereby, you will be able to progressively increase the power of your hands and mobility of your ankle joints and, therefore, you will always be ready to treat anybody, yourself or someone else, whenever a need arises.

(4) As a part of mental preparation, try to gather information about factors that derange health. Find out everything

you can about the disease you are suffering from, about its causes and the organ of the body it is inhabitating. If you wish to launch a war against your disease, you should fully arm yourself with the weapon of knowledge.

After a couple of days of preliminary preparation, described above, you are ready to treat yourself by Reflex Zone Therapy. In Section II of this book, you will find chapters devoted to the treatment of specific disorders. To influence any particular diseased organ, the pressure treatment has to be emphasized on specific area/s on one or both feet.

However, Reflexology believes in a holistic approach to treatment. It contends that no organ of the body can become diseased (or remain healthy) in isolation of other organs. Therefore, the entire soles of both the feet should initially be stimulated for a short time, before concentrating on the specific areas related to the disordered organs. This can be termed **'general treatment of the whole body'.** The easiest method of 'covering' the 'trigger' spots related to all internal organs of the body is to roll the two feet on specially designed long, wooden or plastic rollers for three to five minutes. This produces a pleasant sensation of warmth in the feet and goes a long way in restoring a state of balance (homoeostasis) inside the body.

Fig. 5.4 : Rollers

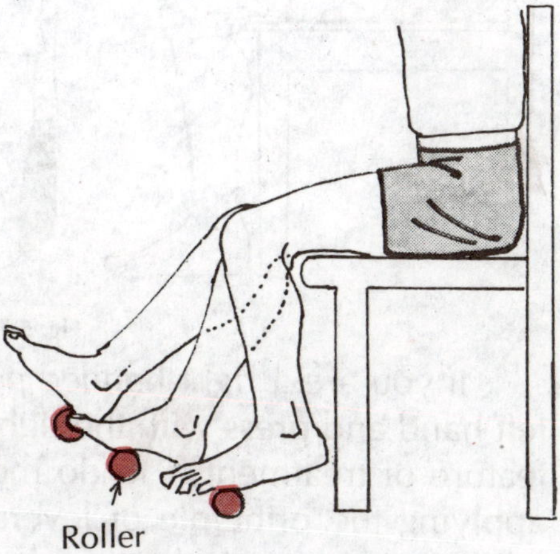

Fig. 5.5

Alternatively, you can wear specially designed 'Reflexology slippers' (or insert 'Reflexology insoles' into your shoes) and walk for a couple of minutes.

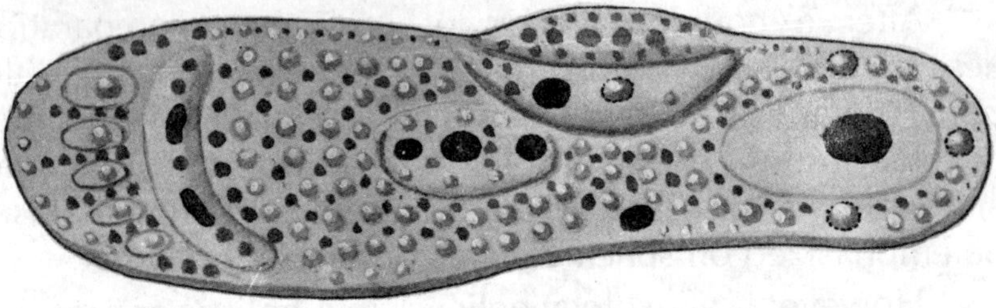

Fig. 5.6 : Reflexology insole

You are now ready for further stimulation of key spots on the soles related to the diseased organ/s as described in Section II of this book.

It is believed that Reflex Zone Therapy should preferably be started with the left foot. Take one of the positions shown below, with the left foot on the right thigh.

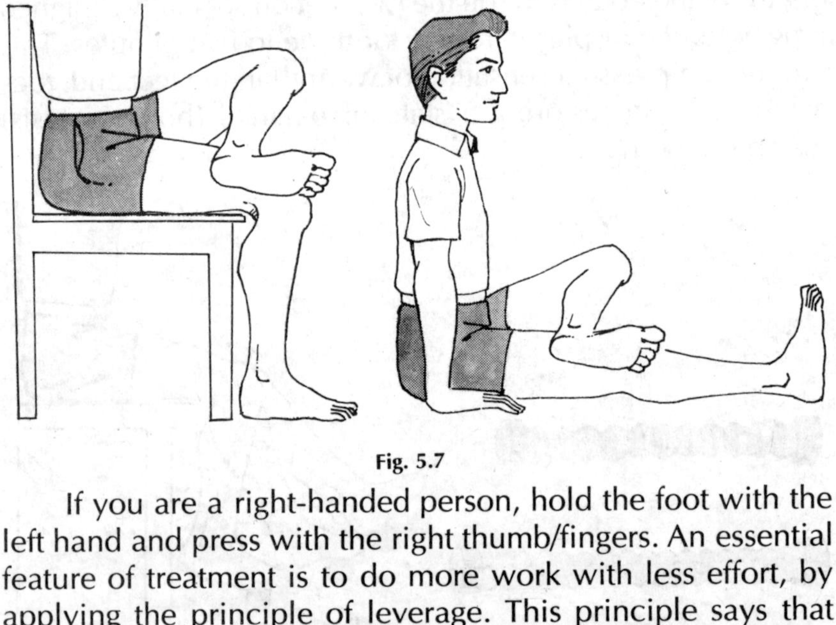

Fig. 5.7

If you are a right-handed person, hold the foot with the left hand and press with the right thumb/fingers. An essential feature of treatment is to do more work with less effort, by applying the principle of leverage. This principle says that while pressing with the thumb-tip, the rest of the palm and fingers should be kept in firm contact with the edge and the dorsum of the foot, as shown in diagrams below :

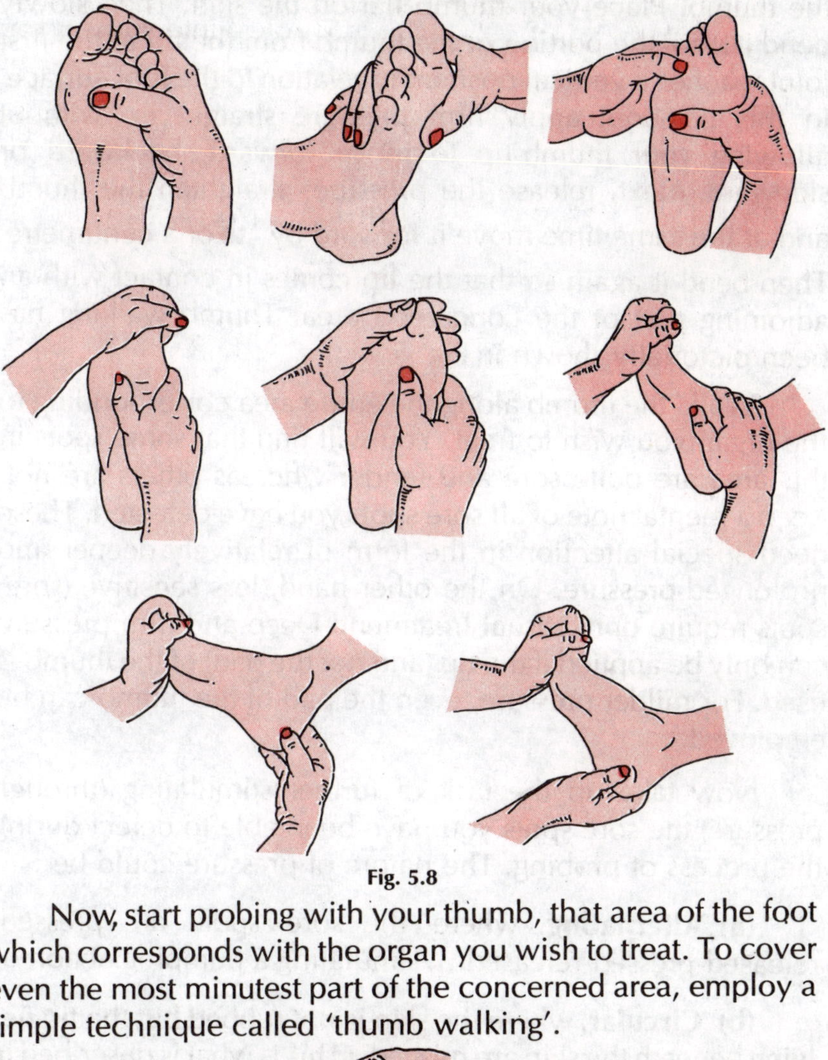

Fig. 5.8

Now, start probing with your thumb, that area of the foot which corresponds with the organ you wish to treat. To cover even the most minutest part of the concerned area, employ a simple technique called 'thumb walking'.

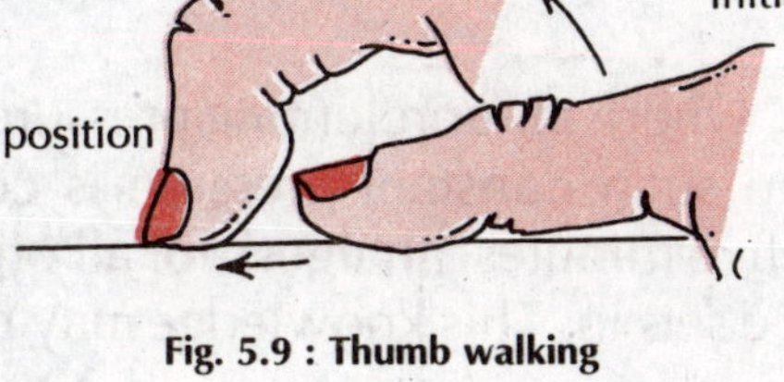

Fig. 5.9 : Thumb walking

This technique is a particular way of holding and moving the thumb. Place your thumb flat on the skin. Then slowly bend it until the portion of the thumb from the tip to the first joint reaches a vertical position in relation to the foot-surface. In this position, apply firm pressure straight in, without allowing your thumb-tip to move forward, backward or sideward. Next, release the pressure, straighten the thumb and at the same time move it forward by $\frac{1}{4}$th of a centimetre. Then bend it again so that the tip comes in contact with an adjoining part of the concerned area. Thumb walking has been pictorially shown in Fig. 5.9.

'Walk' the thumb along the entire area corresponding to the organ you wish to treat. You will find that some spots in this area are quite sore and tender whereas others are not. Keep a mental note of all sore spots you have detected. These need special attention in the form of relatively deeper and prolonged pressure. On the other hand, less sensitive (sore) spots require only casual treatment. Deep and firm pressure can only be applied if the tip (and not the pad) of the thumb is used. For milder pressure, even the pad of the thumb can be employed.

Now take up the task of further stimulating (through pressure) the sore spots you have been able to detect during the process of probing. The nature of pressure could be :

(a) **Alternating**, where the sore spots are pressed-released-pressed-released..., simulating a pumping action **or**

(b) **Circular**, where the skin is not rubbed but the tissues lying beneath the skin are rubbed. (This is what is described in some books as trying to crush 'sugar crystals' lying beneath the skin.) **or**

(c) **Constant**, where an unrelenting pressure is given on a sore spot. When such constant pressure is continued for more than four to five minutes, analgesia of all organs lying in that particular zone sets in. This knowledge may be utilized in the treatment of such painful disorders such as headache, earache, toothache, etc. When long-term constant pressure is required, the thumb is likely to start tiring and aching. To prevent this and to make the work easier, you may use clothes-pins or rubber-bands on toes, as shown in Fig. 5.10.

The use of such gadgets also becomes necessary for persons suffering from some disability of thumb/fingers (e.g., arthritis, muscle-weakness etc.), big belly (which makes reaching the foot difficult) or stiffness of knee and ankle joints.

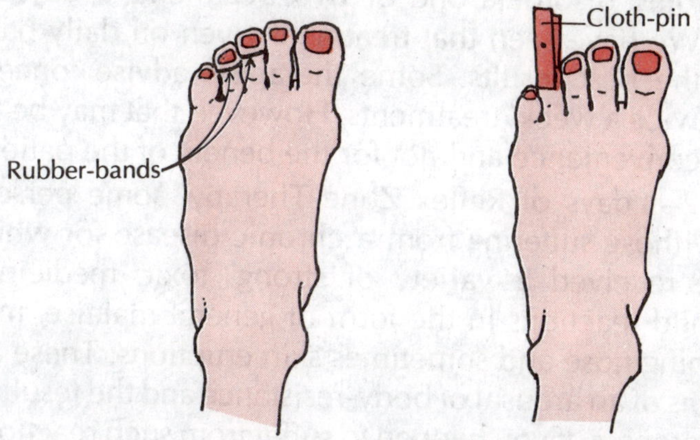

Fig. 5.10

Some books advise against using anything except thumb/finger for pressure. But we maintain that clothes-pins or rubber-bands, too, produce equally good (if not better) results when the need is to relieve pain. Remember : Dr. Fitzgerald, the discoverer of Reflex Zone Therapy, strongly recommended and successfully employed such gadgets.

After giving either alternating or circular or constant pressure on a sore spot for about one minute, move to the neighbouring sore spot. In this manner, cover the entire area on the foot that corresponds with the diseased organ/s. With this, you have completed the treatment of the left foot.

Next take up the stimulation of key, sore spots on the right foot.

While working on either foot, do not press upon corns, callouses, injured or cracked areas and varicosed veins. Instead, corresponding spots on the palms may be utilized.

After finishing pressure treatment of both the feet, if possible, take rest by lying down for 5-10 minutes.

In acute disorders like high fever, intense headache, acute bronchitis, etc, pressure treatment needs frequent repetition i.e., every 2-3 hours. The frequency may be reduced as the condition improves.

In chronic disorders, one or two treatments a day are sufficient. We have seen that treatment given on daily basis produces the best results. Some therapists advise 'once a week' or 'twice a week' treatments. However, that may be for their own convenience and not for the benefit of the patient.

After 2–3 days of Reflex Zone Therapy, some persons (especially those suffering from a chronic disease for which they have received a variety of strong, toxic medicines) develop mild reactions in the form of general malaise, mild fever, running nose and sometimes skin eruptions. These are merely signs of an arousal of body-resistance and the resultant cleansing process. If you happen to suffer from such reactions, don't panic. These reactions subside on their own if you take complete bed-rest and abstain from taking food for a couple of days. However, continue to receive pressure therapy and consume a lot of water (or other light fluids).

Finally, let us take up the issue of good time to treat. We will say that, in general, treatment can be had at any time of the day. However, refrain from treating yourself immediately after you have had a heavy meal. Try to keep a uniform time-gap between every two treatments.

Regularity is extremely essential for successful Reflexology treatment. However, the fast modern life leaves people with little time for Reflexology. We have been told, time and again, by people that they are not able to be regular with treatment, simply because they forget. Fitting Reflexology in the daily schedule is not easy for the city people who are always on the run. If you, too, are one of them, you will have to **create** time for Reflexology. You can do other things and still work on your feet. You may stimulate key spots on your feet (a) while travelling to work or back home, (b) while watching television, (c) while reading a newspaper in the morning or (d) while talking to family-members, friends or on phone. Keeping a foot-roller under the dining table or the office table makes it possible to stimulate key areas related to various organs of the body while eating or working. Do this for a few days and soon you will find yourself doing it almost unconsciously!

PART II

6. REFLEXOLOGY IN PAINFUL DISORDERS

HEADACHE

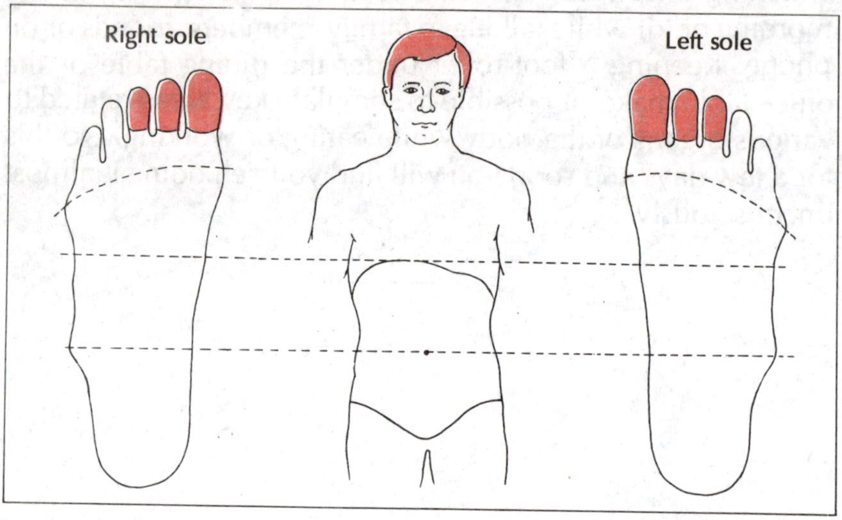

Fig. 6.1

Headache tops the list of common scourges of mankind. It is so common that everybody suffers from it at some time or another. When the problem becomes chronic and recurrent, life becomes miserable.

Medicines and 'over-the-counter' pills worth millions of rupees are purchased every year by the victims of headache. However, none of them is absolutely safe, especially when consumed over a prolonged period.

Common causes and features of headache have been tabulated below.

	Cause / Type	Distinguishing features
1	Mental tension, resulting into tension of facial, scalp and neck muscles	Victim admits to be facing unfavourable circumstances and of possessing a worrying nature. Headache is usually mild and may be located anywhere : front, top or back of the head.
2	Colds and sinusitis	Victim gives a history of colds, which have gone to the head! Severe pain usually in the forehead or about the eyes, which gets worse on stooping or coughing.

	Cause/Type	Distinguishing features
3	Visual problems	Mild pain in the forehead, occuring only after the eyes have been used, for hours together, in tasks requiring a lot of concentration. Headache is relieved if eyes are rested for a while.
4	Migraine	Vascular headache, usually affecting one half of the head; cause is unknown but some consider it psychological. Pain is very severe and many a time subsides only after a bout of vomitting.

Reflex Zone Therapy :

(A) General treatment of the whole body : Start with general treatment as detailed on Page 33

(B) Specific treatment of the head : The head is represented chiefly on the two big toes. Place the left foot on the right thigh. Steady this foot with the left hand. Now start 'walking' your right thumb over the left big toe, in small steps, taking care not to omit even a smallest spot. During such probing, every time you encounter a sore spot, stop moving the thumb further and with its tip give deep alternating pressure for about a minute.

After covering the entire left big toe (including its sides), reverse the positions of the legs and in a similar manner stimulate the trigger area for the head on the right big toe.

For chronic or recurrent headache, repeat this treatment twice a day.

(C) For very severe headache : Tie small rubber-bands on both big toes (or all toes) for 10-12 minutes. During this period, if the toes turn black or start paining, remove the rubber-bands for a while (till the normal colour returns) and then tie them again.

Note : If the headache tends to recur, the underlying cause should be sought and treated.

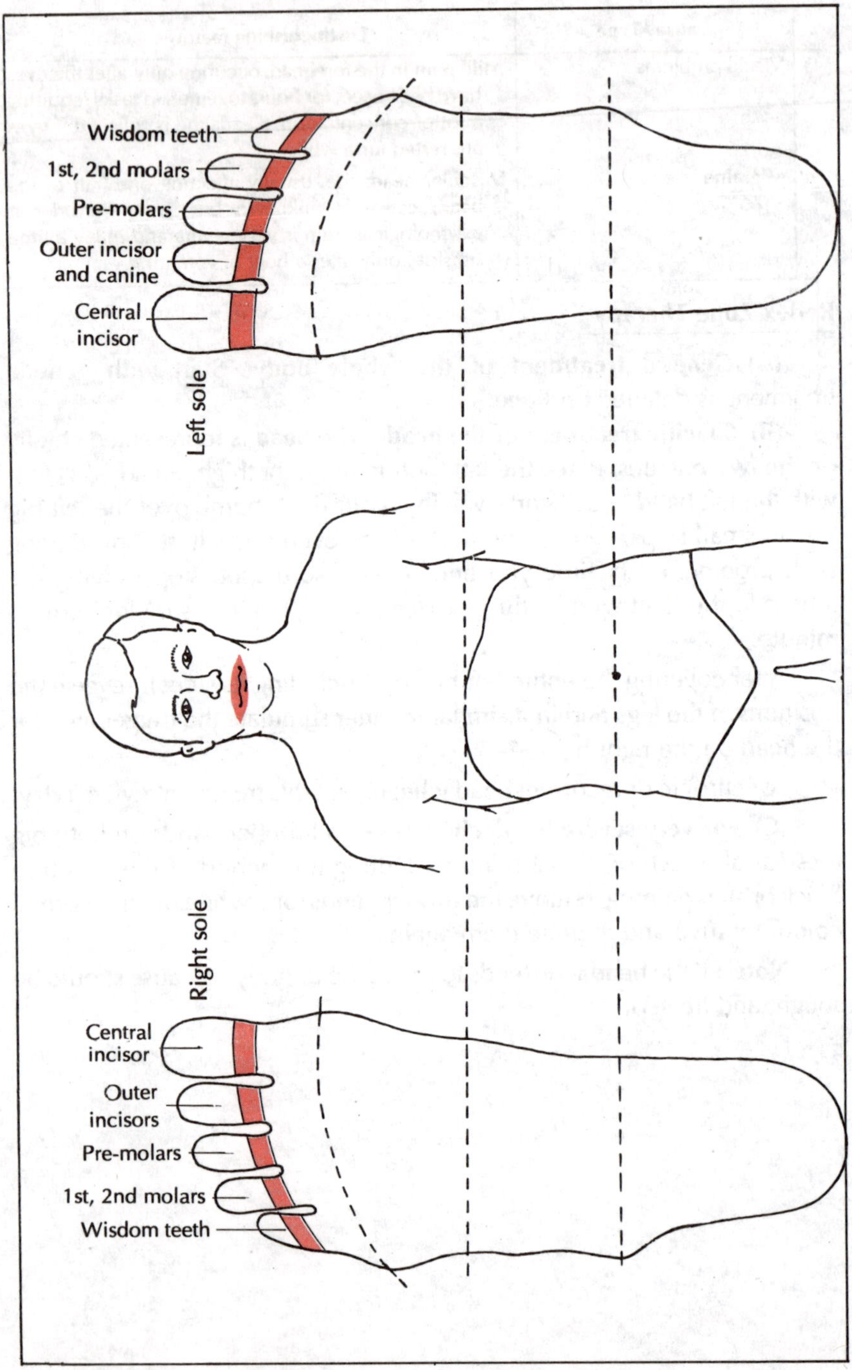
Wisdom teeth
1st, 2nd molars
Pre-molars
Outer incisor and canine
Central incisor
Left sole
Right sole
Central incisor
Outer incisors
Pre-molars
1st, 2nd molars
Wisdom teeth

Fig. 6.2

TOOTHACHE

Only a person who has suffered from toothache knows how bad it can be. Indeed, it drives a person to despair.

Most adults have 32 permanent teeth, 16 on each jaw. Of these 32 teeth, there are 8 incisors (sharp, chisel-like teeth meant for cutting), 4 canine (pointed teeth meant for tearing or gripping), 8 premolars and 12 molars (meant for grinding).

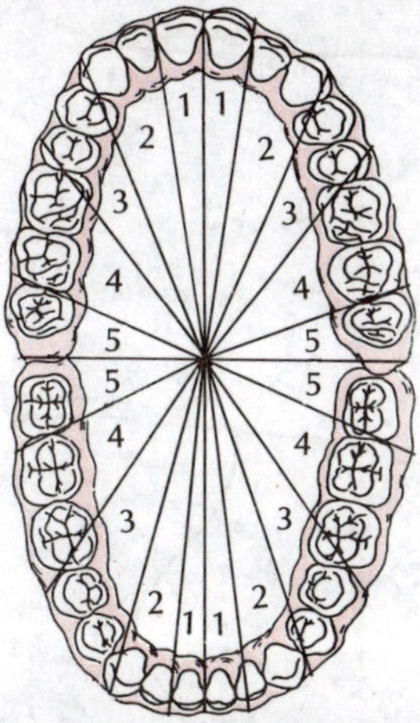

Fig. 6.3 : The teeth

The central incisors lie in zone 1.

The outer incisors and the canine teeth lie in zone 2.

The premolars lie in zone 3.

The first and the second molars lie in zone 4.

The third molar (wisdom) teeth lie in zone 5.

Reflex Zone Therapy :

(A) General treatment of the whole body : Start with general treatment as described on page 33.

(B) Specific treatment of the affected tooth : The teeth are represented on the basal parts of the toes as shown in the adjoining diagram. Pinch the toe that corresponds to your aching tooth and give deep, alternating (or constant) pressure for 2 minutes or more. Repeat frequently till the pain is relieved.

(C) For excruciating toothache : Tie a small rubber-band on the corresponding toe for 10-12 minutes. During this period, if the toe starts aching or turns black, remove the rubber-band for a while (till the normal colour returns) and then tie it again. If necessary, repeat again after an hour or two.

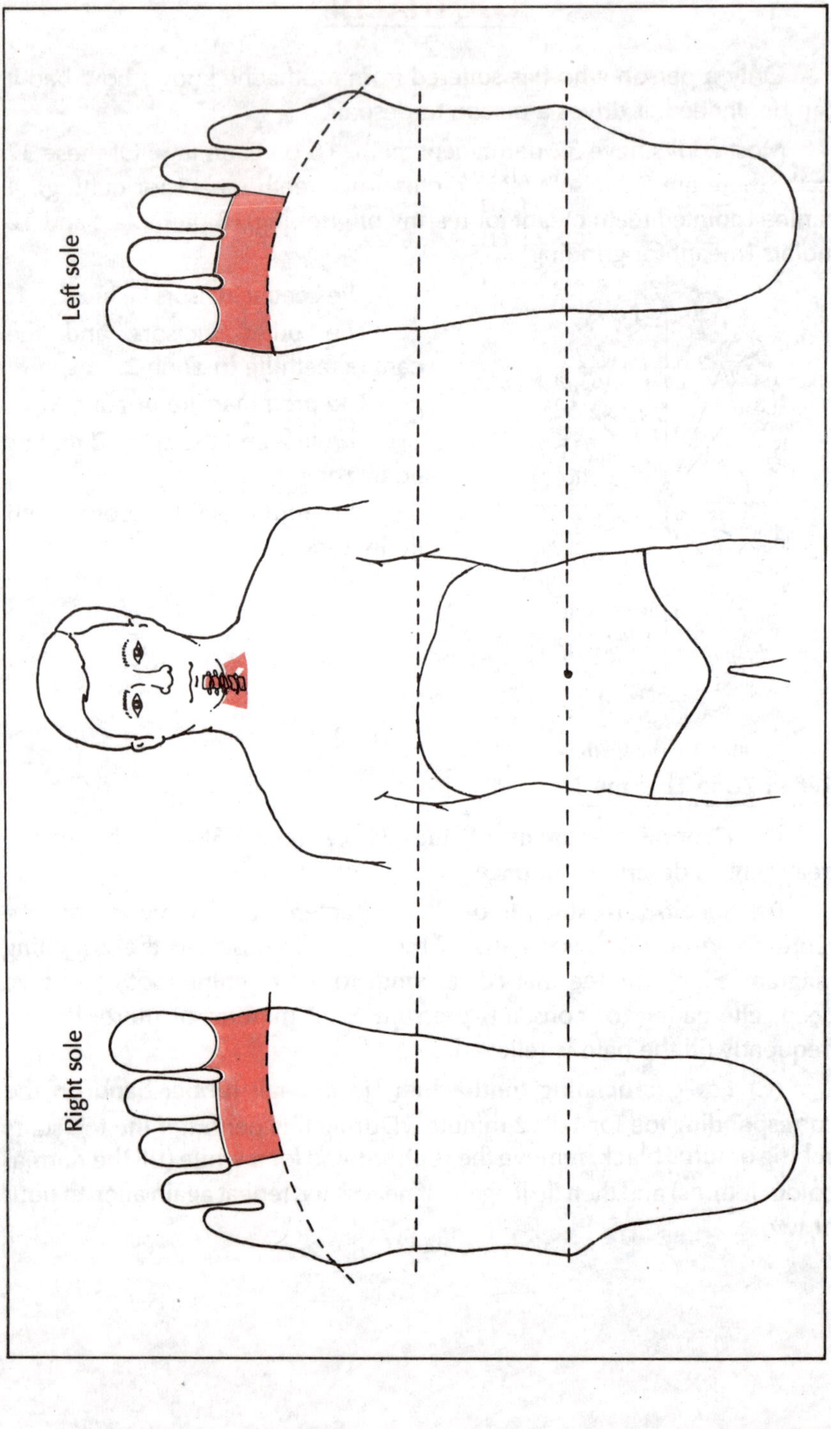

Fig. 6.4

PROBLEMS OF THE NECK

Stiffness; Pain; Cervical Spondylosis

Our neck region has seven 'cervical' vertebrae which are considerably mobile, allowing us to nod our head to say 'yes' or shake our head to say 'no'. This excessive flexibility renders the neck region vulnerable to muscle sprains and arthritis.

Osteoarthritis of the joints between the vertebrae of the neck has been given a special name : **cervical spondylosis.** People moving around with broad collars around their necks is a common sight. These are the people suffering from cervical spondylosis.

Reflex Zone Therapy :

(A) General treatment of the whole body : Start with general treatment as described on page 33.

(B) Specific treatment of the neck : The neck is represented chiefly on the big toes (and, to some extent, also on the second and the third toes) as shown in the adjoining diagram. Place the left foot on the right thigh. Steady this foot with the left hand. Now, start 'walking' your right thumb over the trigger areas for the neck, in small steps, taking care not to omit even a smallest spot. During such probing, every time you encounter a sore spot, stop moving the thumb further and with its tip give deep alternating pressure for about a minute.

Next, reverse the positions of the legs and in a similar manner stimulate the trigger areas for the neck on the right foot.

Repeat this treatment twice a day.

(C) The narrow portion at the root of the big toe corresponds to the neck. Holding the big toe and rotating it (both clockwise and anti-clockwise) about the foot is equivalent to rotating the head about the body. This proves useful in relieving the stiffness of the neck. This manoeuvre, too, can be repeated twice a day.

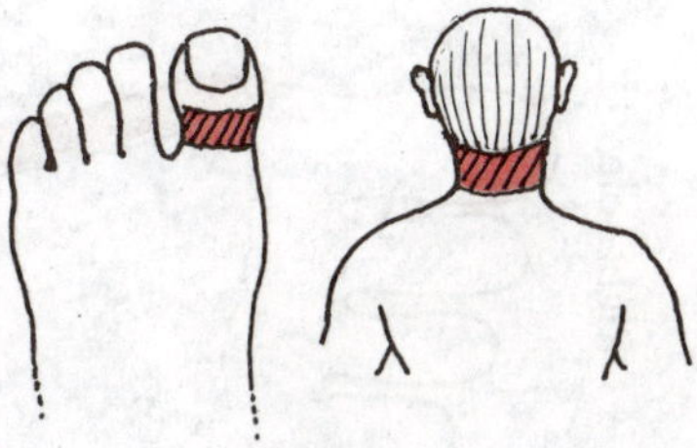

Fig. 6.5

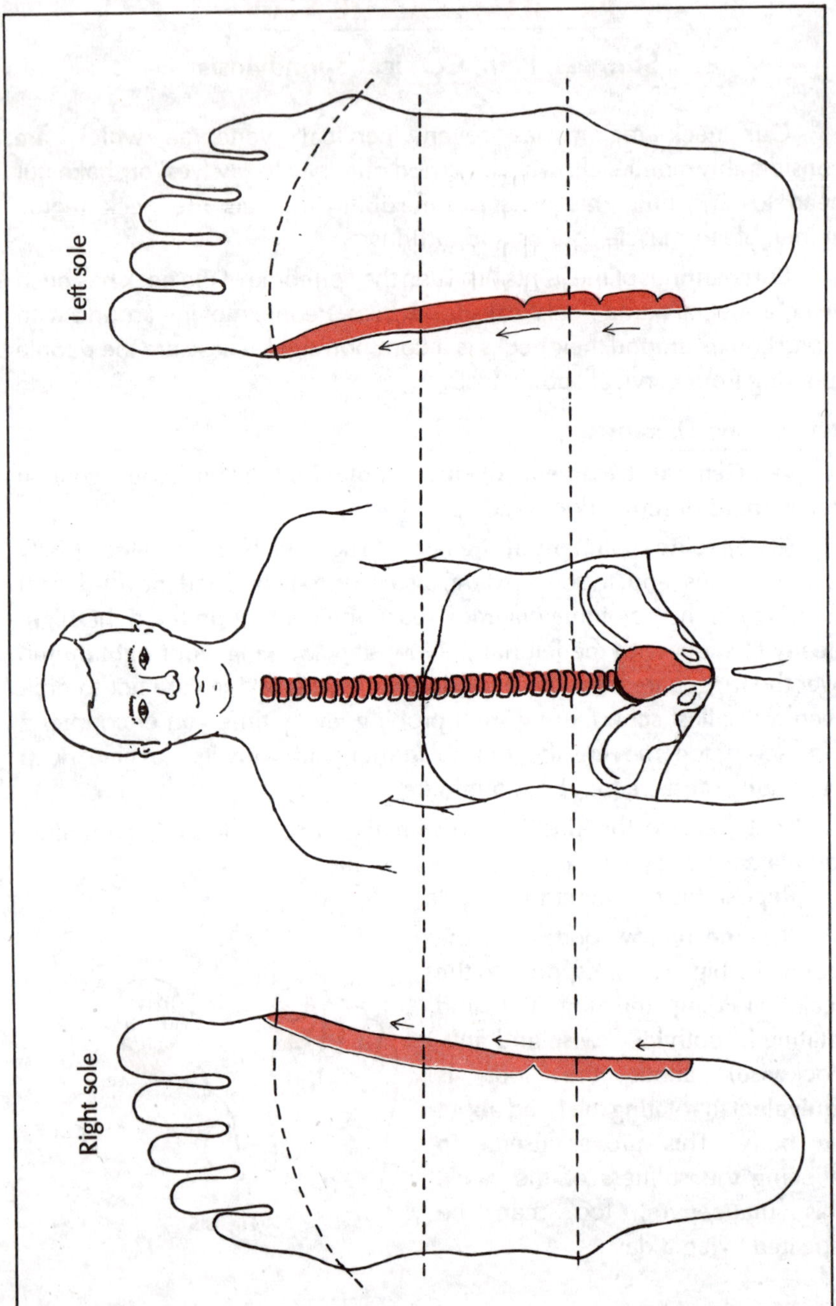

Fig. 6.6

PROBLEMS OF THE BACK (SPINE)

Pain; Stiffness; Lumbago; Sciatica

Perhaps with the exception of headache, backache is the most common scourge of mankind. Very few people complete their lives without experiencing backache in one form or the other. It may just be a temporary inconvenience that comes and goes; or it may interfere continuously and relentlessly with work, rest and sleep.

More often than not, backache is the result of a 'spasm' of weak back muscles. Occasionally, it is caused by arthritis of vertebral joints or a 'slipping' of an inter-vertebral disc.

The spine is represented along the medial (inner) edge of each foot (see the adjoining diagram). A disorder of a particular (e.g., thoracic, lumbar, sacral or coccygeal) part of the spine is reflected (in the form of soreness) in the corresponding part of the foot-edge.

Reflex Zone Therapy :

(A) General treatment for the whole body : Start with general treatment as described on page 33.

(B) Specific treatment of the back : As shown in the adjoining diagram, the spine is represented on the inner edges of the two feet. Place the left foot on the right thigh. Steady this foot with the left hand. Now, starting from the heel, 'walk' your thumb forward along the inner border of foot, in small steps, taking care not to omit even a smallest spot. During such probing, every time you encounter a sore spot, stop moving the thumb further and with its tip give deep alternating pressure for about a minute.

Next, reverse the positions of the legs and in a similar manner, stimulate the trigger areas for the back on the inner border of the right foot.

Repeat this treatment twice a day.

(C) For very severe, incapacitating backache : Tie small rubber-bands on both big toes for 10-12 minutes. During this period, if the toes start paining or turn black, remove the bands for a while (till the normal colour is restored) and then apply them again. If necessary, repeat this treatment again after an hour or two.

Suggested reading : Backache– Prevention and Cure' by the same authors.

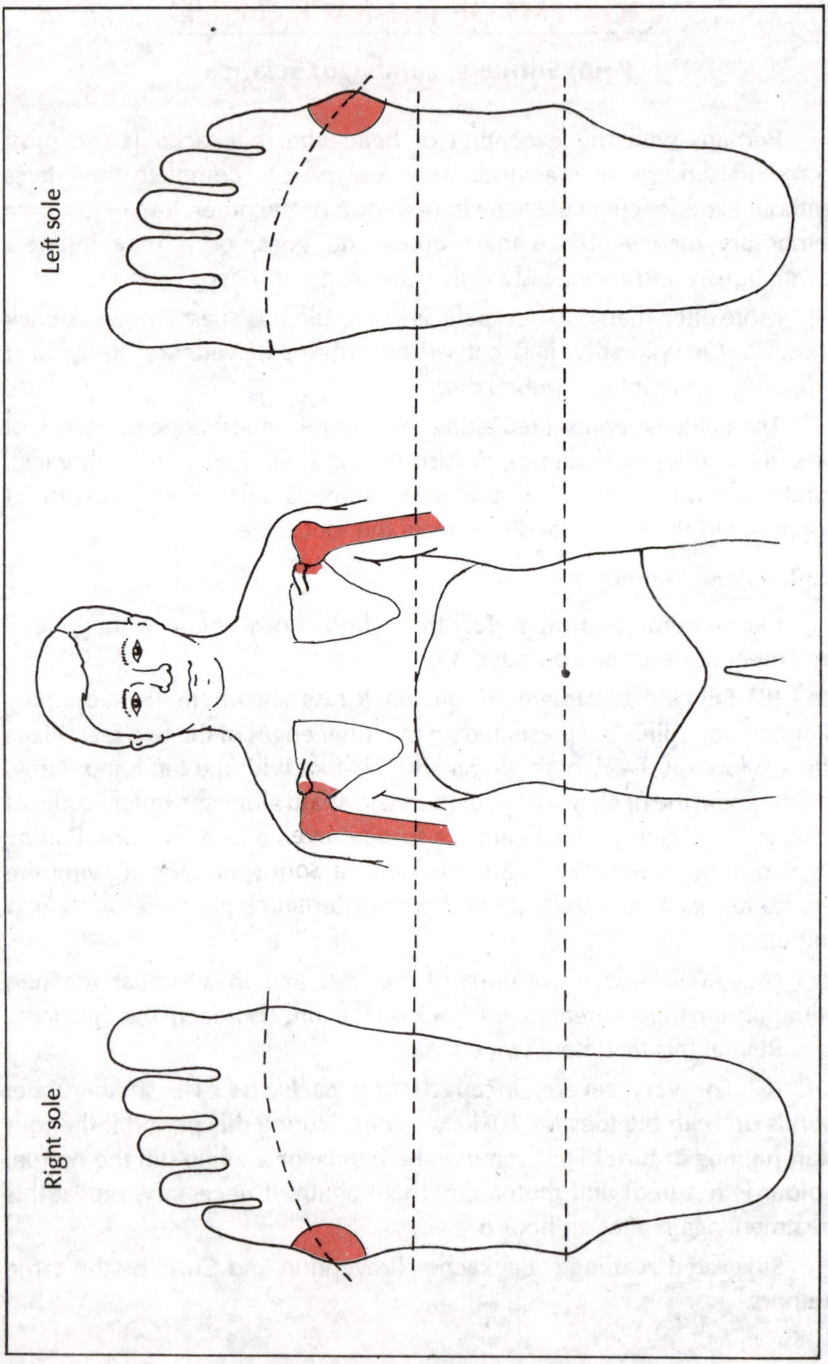

Fig. 6.7

PROBLEMS OF THE SHOULDER

Stiffness; Pain; Frozen Shoulder

Shoulder joint is the joint between the head of the humerus (upper end of the arm bone) and the glenoid cavity of the scapula (the triangular bone of the upper back).

Since it is a 'ball and socket' type of joint, it allows a great deal of movement. This excessive mobility makes it vulnerable to sprains.

A very common disorder of this joint is **'Frozen shoulder'** or **Peri-arthritis of the shoulder'**. This is characterized by severe stiffness of the shoulder. All possible movements are equally restricted and any effort to move the arm produces severe pain.

Shoulder may also develop osteo-arthritis, especially if it has been, previously, a victim of injury. However, osteo-arthritis of the shoulder is much less common than that of joints of the lower limbs.

Reflex Zone Therapy :

(A) General treatment of the whole body : Start with general treatment as described on page 33.

(B) Specific treatment of the shoulder : The right shoulder is represented on the outer border of the right foot, whereas the left shoulder is represented on the outer border of the left foot, as shown in the adjoining diagram.

Place the corresponding foot on the other thigh. 'Walk' the thumb over the entire trigger area for the shoulder in small steps, taking care not to omit even a smallest spot. During such probing, every time you encounter a sore spot, stop moving the thumb further and, with its tip, give deep, alternating pressure for about a minute. Repeat this treatment twice a day.

(C) For very severe pain : Tie small rubber-bands on all the toes (or fingers) of the corresponding side for 10-12 minutes. During this period, if a toe starts aching or turns black, remove the concerned band for a while (till the normal colour returns) and then reapply it. If necessary, repeat again after an hour or two.

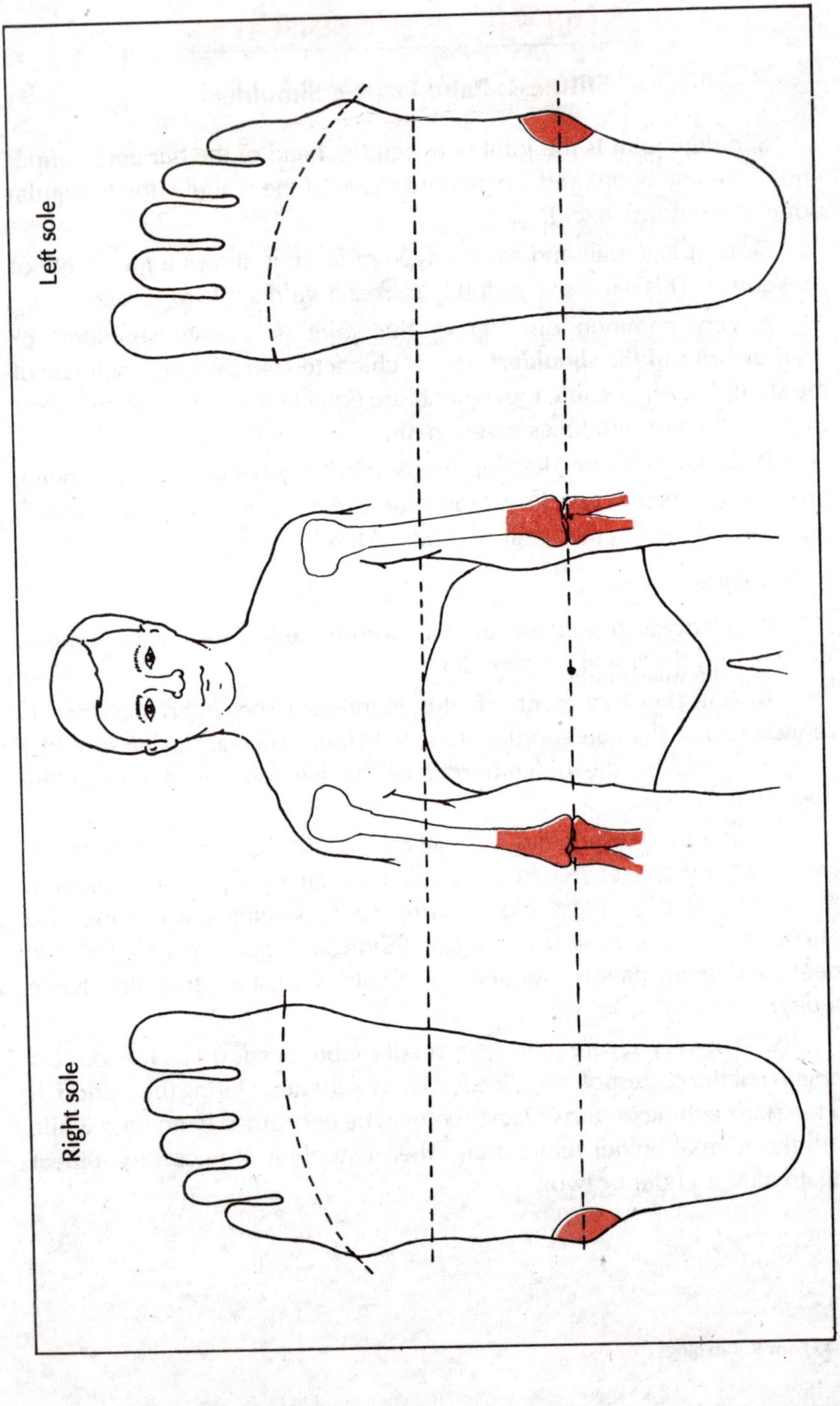

Fig. 6.8

PROBLEMS OF THE ELBOW

Stiffness; Pain; Arthritis; Tennis Elbow

Elbow joint, like the knee joint, is a hinge type of joint present between the lower end of the arm bone (humerus) and the upper ends of forearm bones (radius and ulna).

This joint allows movement only in one plane. Therefore, it is less likely to suffer from sprains.

Among common disorders of the elbow are : **tennis elbow, osteo-arthritis** and other forms of **arthritis.** Symptoms of these disorders include pain and/or stiffness in the elbow.

Reflex Zone Therapy :

(A) General treatment of the entire body : Start with general treatment as described on page 33.

(B) Specific treatment of the elbow : The right elbow is represented on the outer border of the right foot whereas the left elbow is represented on the outer border of the left foot as shown in the adjoining diagram.

Place the corresponding foot on the other thigh. 'Walk' the thumb over the entire trigger area for the elbow in small steps, taking care not to omit even a smallest spot. During such probing, every time you encounter a sore spot, stop moving the thumb further and, with its tip, give deep, alternating pressure for about a minute. Repeat this treatment twice a day.

(C) For very severe pain : Tie small rubber-bands on all the toes (or fingers) of the corresponding side for 10-12 minutes. During this period, if a toe starts paining or turns black, remove the concerned band for a while (till the normal colour returns) and then reapply it. If necessary, repeat again after an hour or two.

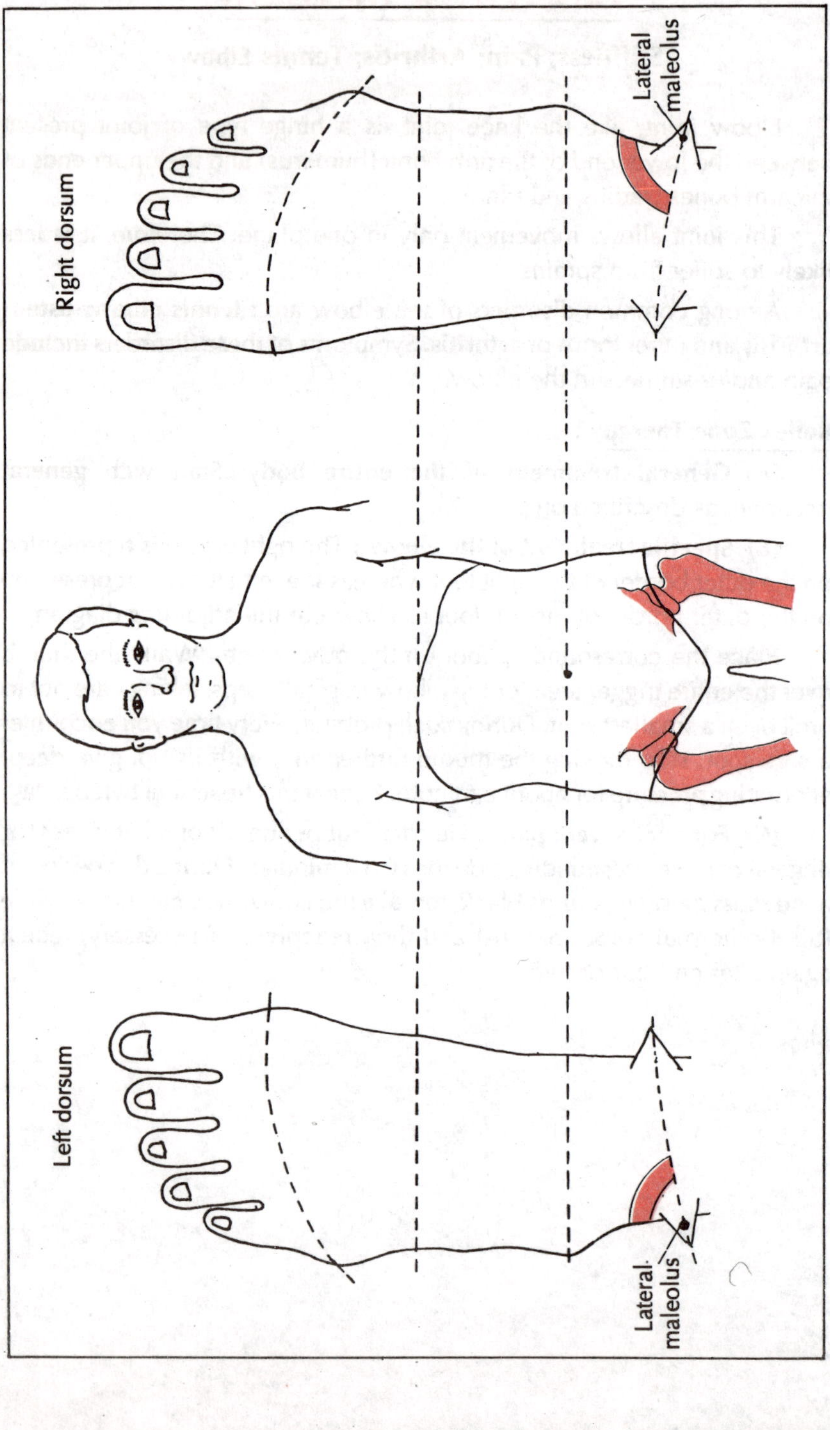
Right dorsum
Lateral maleolus
Left dorsum
Lateral maleolus

Fig. 6.9

PROBLEMS OF THE HIP JOINT

Pain; Stiffness; Arthritis

Like the shoulder, the hip is a 'ball and socket' variety of joint between the upper end of the thigh bone (femur) and the acetabular cavity of the pelvic bone.

It affords a wide range of movement in various directions. This excessive mobility makes the joint vulnerable to sprains.

Hip joint is also, frequently, a victim of various forms of **arthritis,** rendering it painful and stiff.

Reflex Zone Therapy :

(A) General treatment of the whole body : Start with general treatment as described on page 33.

(B) Specific treatment of the hip : As shown in the adjoining diagram, the hip is represented on the front and the outer surfaces of the corresponding ankle, around a prominent bone called the lateral maleolus.

'Walk' your thumb (or a finger) over the trigger area for the affected hip, in small steps, taking care not to omit even a smallest spot. During such probing, every time you encounter a sore spot, stop moving the finger further and with its tip give deep, alternating pressure for about a minute. Repeat this treatment twice a day.

(C) For very severe pain : Tie small rubber-bands on all the toes of the corresponding foot for 10-12 minutes. During this period, if a toe starts aching or turns blue remove the concerned band for a while (till the normal colour returns) and then reapply it. If necessary, repeat again after an hour or two.

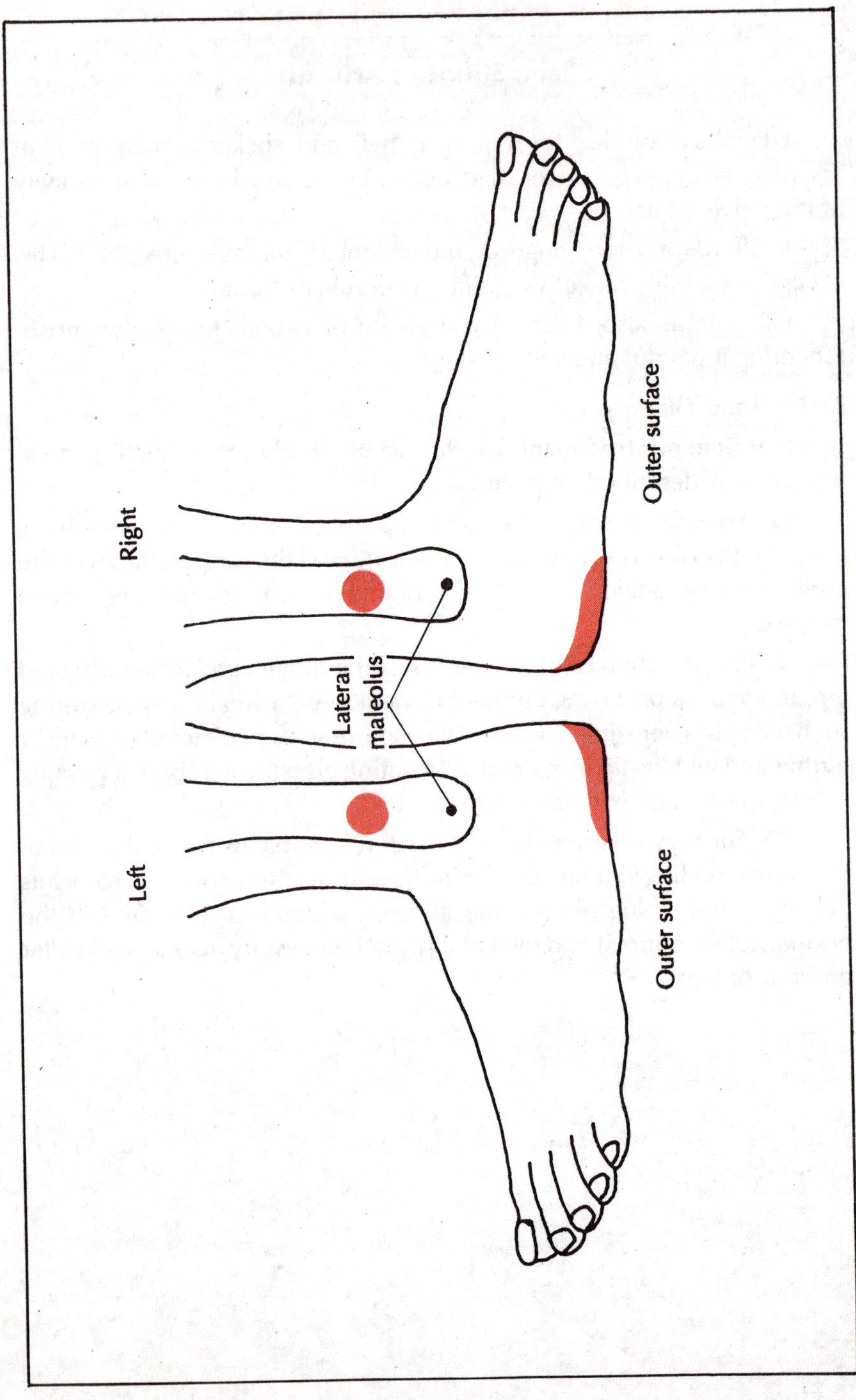

Fig. 6.10

PROBLEMS OF THE KNEE JOINT

Pain; Stiffness; Arthritis

Like the elbow, even the knee is a hinge type of joint between the lower end of the thigh bone (femur) and the upper end of the leg bone (tibia). This joint allows movement only in one plane.

Having to bear a greater part of the body-weight, the knee joint becomes a victim of wear and tear leading to **'osteo-arthritis'.** Obese people and athletes start suffering from this problem early in their lives.

Other forms of arthritis may also affect the knee. Osteo-arthritis can be differentiated from these by (1) an absence of swelling, redness or warmth over the joint, (2) presence of a crackling noise (crepitus) when the joint is moved and (3) presence of characteristic 'osteophytes' at the edges of the joint, visualized on a X-ray picture.

Reflex Zone Therapy :

(A) General treatment of the entire body : Start with general treatment as described on page 33.

(B) Specific treatment of the knee : At the outer aspect of the ankle is a prominent bone called the lateral maleolus. Starting from the lateral maleolus, 'walk' your thumb upward till you reach a sensitive spot. For **acute problems of the knee,** give deep, alternating pressure on this spot for about 2 minutes. Repeat this treatment twice a day.

The outer edge of the heel can be utilized to treat **chronic problems of the knee.** 'Walk' your thumb along this narrow area in small steps, taking care not to omit even a small spot. During such probing, every time you encounter a sore spot, stop moving the thumb further and with its tip give deep, alternating pressure for about a minute. Repeat this treatment twice a day.

(C) For very severe pain : Tie small rubber-bands on all toes of the concerned foot for 10-12 minutes. During this period, if a toe starts aching or turns black, remove the concerned rubber-band for a while (till the normal colour returns) and then reapply it. If necessary, repeat after an hour.

7. REFLEXOLOGY IN DISORDERS OF THE RESPIRATORY SYSTEM

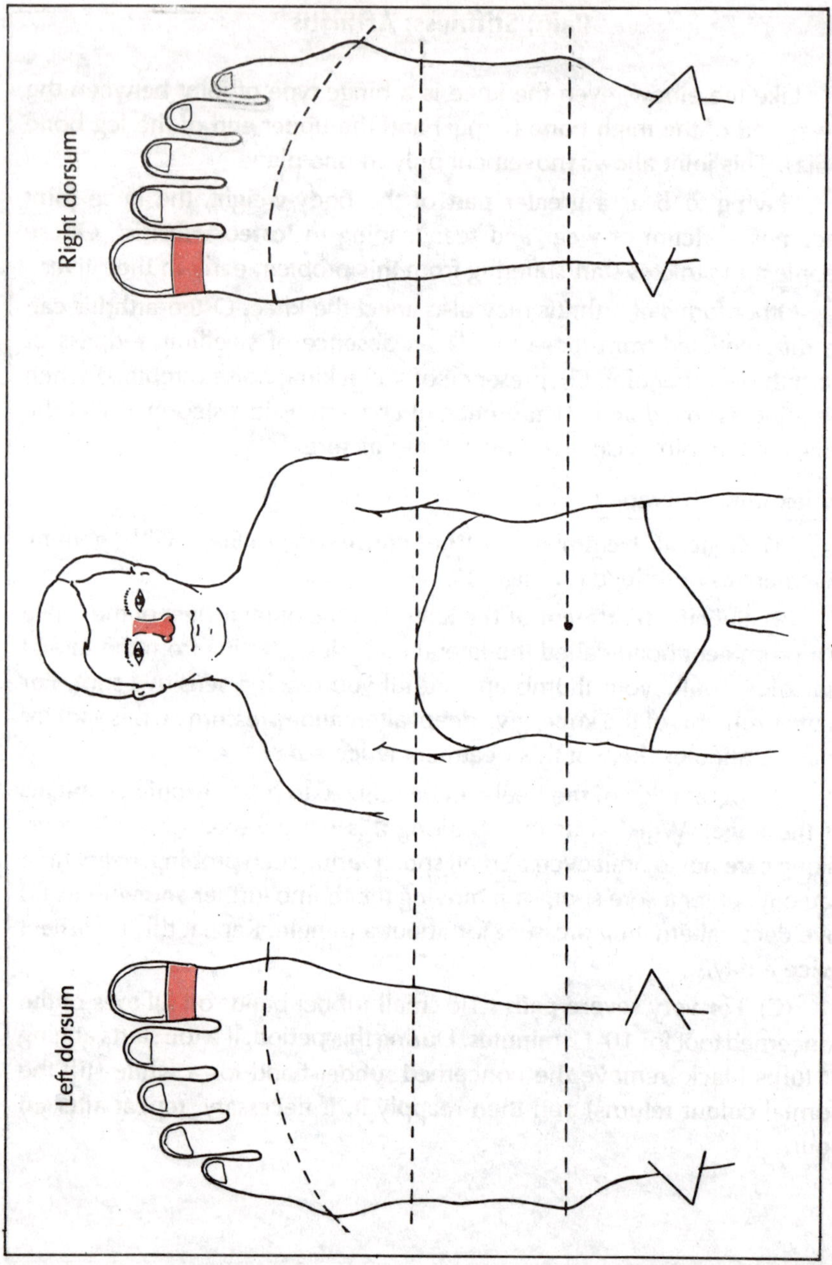

Fig. 7.1

PROBLEMS OF THE NOSE

Colds; Blockage of Nose

In India, the nose enjoys a place of pride among all organs.

It constitutes the first part of the respiratory system. It filters, warms and moistens the air before allowing it to enter the lungs. And, of course, it enables us to perceive those mouth-watering smells, that emanate from a kitchen.

Unfortunately, the nose is often the victim of an ailment called '**common cold**'. Cold is a viral infection of the inner surface of the nose characterized by sneezing and discharge of a watery or thick fluid, which also blocks the nose. Though not a serious disease, cold causes a lot of discomfort, misery and embarrassment to the sufferer. It is admitted even by doctors that 'cold takes full seven days to get cured; but if treated with medicines, it takes just one week!' However, experience has shown that Reflex Zone Therapy can cut short the duration of a cold.

Reflex Zone Therapy :

(A) General treatment of the whole body : Start with general treatment as described on page 33.

(B) Specific treatment of the nose : As shown in the adjoining diagram, the nose is represented on the dorsum of each big toe, at the base of the nail. Using the thumb (on the upper surface of the big toe) and the index finger (on the lower surface of the big toe) deeply press upon the trigger area for the nose in an alternating manner for about 2 minutes.

In a similar manner, stimulate the trigger area for the nose on the other foot.

Repeat this treatment twice a day.

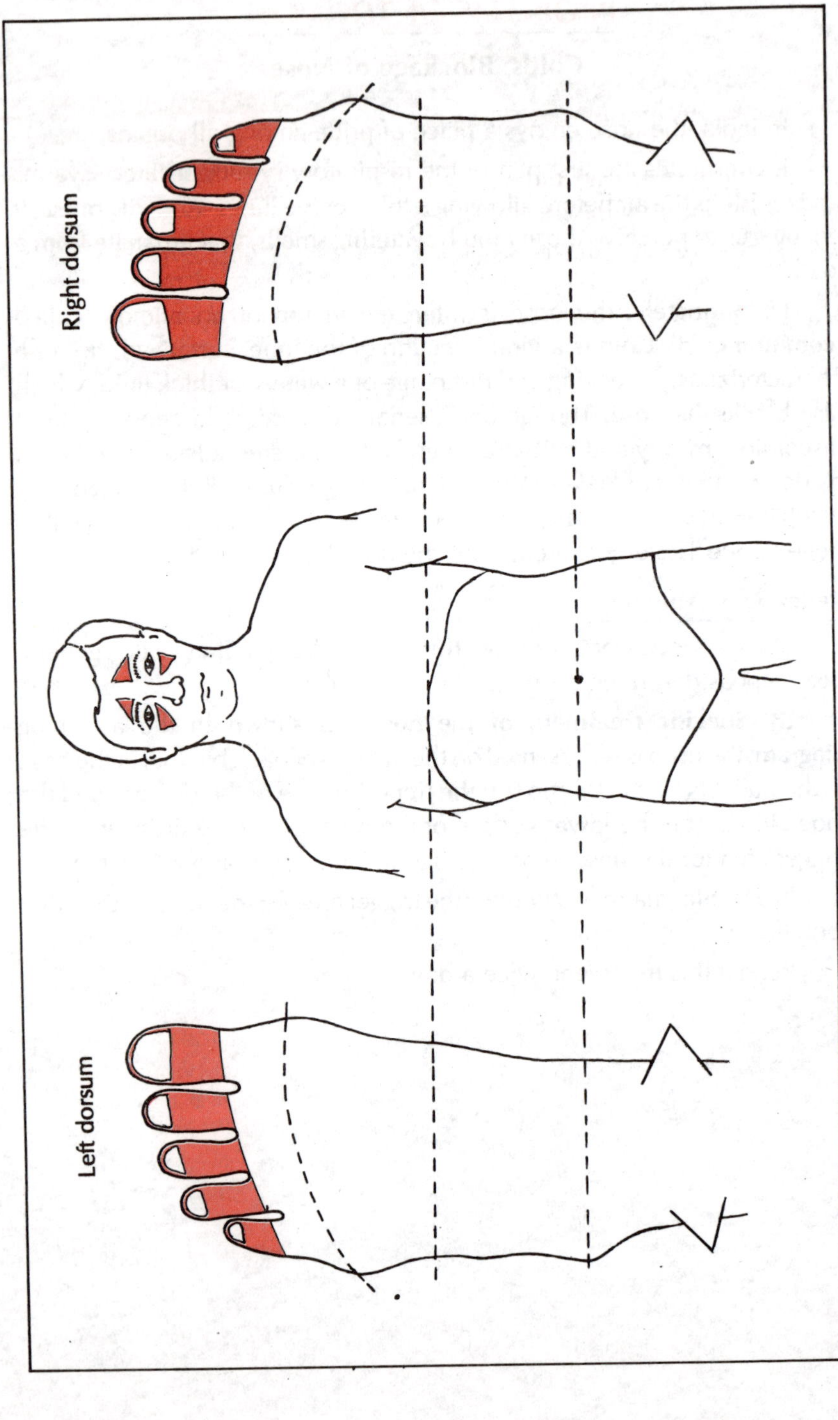

Fig. 7.2

SINUSITIS

Sinuses are air-filled cavities present in the skull bone. If the skull bone were solid, its weight would have been so much as would make even lifting of the head difficult. Thus, sinuses are Nature's means of rendering the skull light-weighted.

Sinuses communicate with the nose through tiny openings. Therefore, a nasal infection sometimes spreads to one or more sinuses, causing a swelling of their inner surfaces. This is termed **sinusitis.**

Symptoms of sinusitis include–

1. Pain in the forehead (in case of frontal sinusitis) or in the cheek (in case of maxillary sinusitis). This pain, which is quite severe, is made worse by stooping, moving the head or coughing. Moreover, it may radiate into the ear, the eye or the teeth.

2. A visible swelling of the skin overlying the concerned sinus.

Reflex Zone Therapy :

(A) General treatment of the entire body : Start with general treatment as described on page 33.

(B) Specific treatment of the sinuses : The sinuses are represented on the upper surfaces of all toes as shown in the adjoining diagram.

Place the left foot on the right thigh. With the thumb and the index finger, pinch each toe and press in an alternating manner for about a minute. Then, reverse the positions of the legs and similarly stimulate the trigger areas for the sinuses on the right foot.

Repeat this treatment twice a day.

(C) For very severe pain : Tie small rubber-bands on the two big toes (or all toes) for 10-12 minutes. During this period, if a toe starts paining or turns black, remove the concerned band for a while (till the normal colour returns) and then reapply it. If necessary, repeat after an hour.

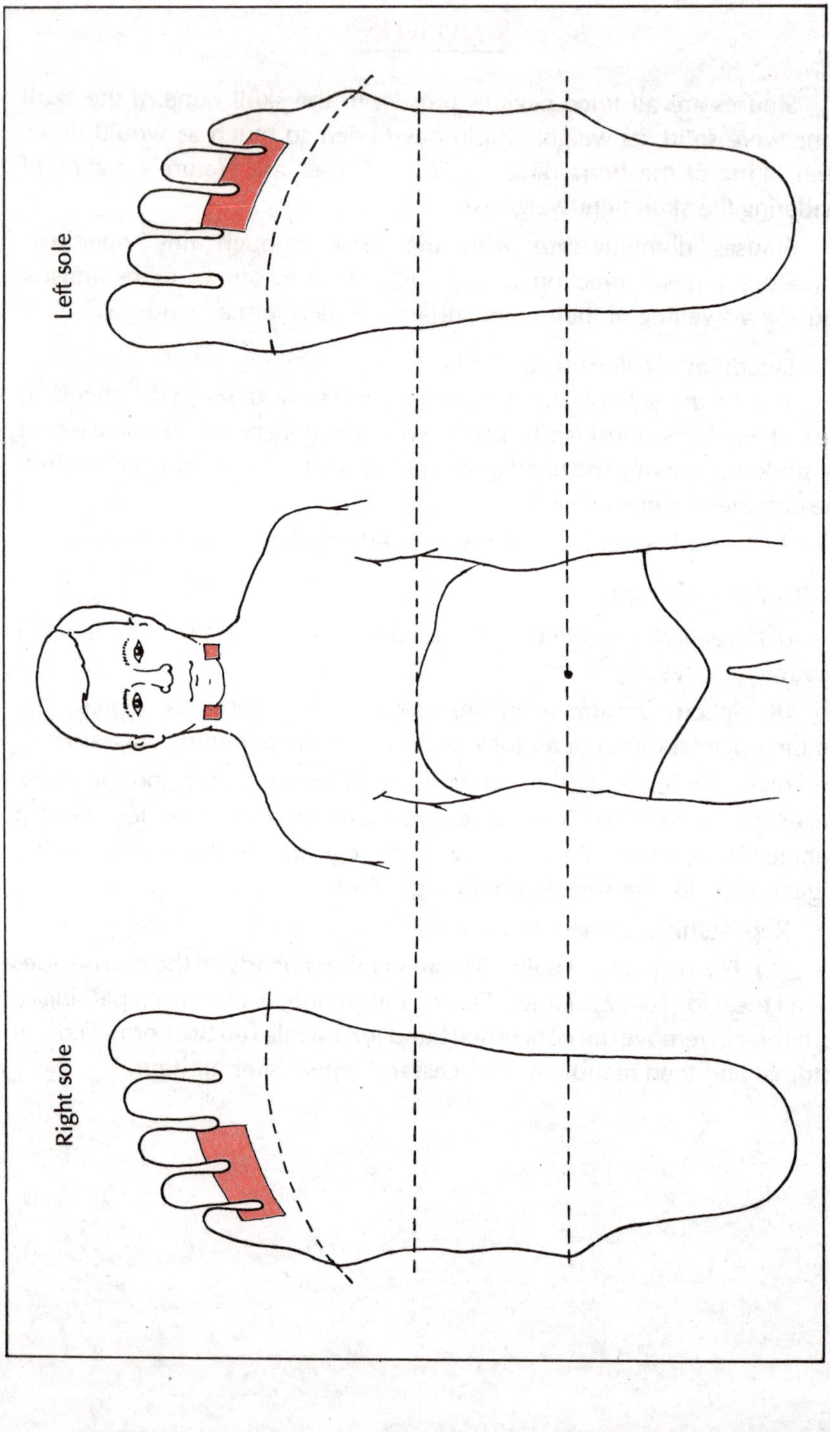

Fig. 7.3

TONSILLITIS

Tonsils are small masses of lymphoid tissues, one lying on either side of the back of the mouth. They work like guards, intercepting all micro-organisms (bacteria, viruses, etc.) that happen to enter the nose or the mouth and preventing them from going deeper into the body. In turn, the tonsils themselves become inflammed (termed **tonsillitis**) causing pain in the throat, difficulty in swallowing and sometimes fever.

Tonsillitis is mainly a childhood problem, seen only occasionally in adults.

A common way of treating swollen tonsils is to remove them by surgery. This operation, called tonsillectomy, is considered the bread and butter of ENT surgeons. Indeed, millions of tonsillectomies are performed every year by doctors who make gullible parents to believe that tonsils are potent sources of infection and unless removed, may cause repeated attacks of colds, cough, sore throat, etc. In cities, very few children reach their teens with the tonsils intact. However, numerous studies conducted world-wide have shown that there is no reduction in the incidences of colds and cough in children without tonsils as compared to children with tonsils.

In conclusion, we would affirm that tonsils are not useless unlike the appendix. In fact, they serve a protective function. If they are removed, your child's first line of defence against infection is lost forever.

Reflex Zone Therapy :

(A) General treatment of the whole body : Start with general treatment as described on page 33.

(B) Specific treatment of the tonsils : The tonsils are represented chiefly at the bases of the 3rd (middle) and the 4th toes as shown in the adjoining diagram.

Place the left foot on the right thigh. With the thumb and the index finger, press the bases of the middle and the 4th toes, each for about a minute, in an alternating manner.

Then, reverse the positions of the legs and similarly stimulate the trigger areas for the tonsils on the right foot.

Repeat this treatment twice a day.

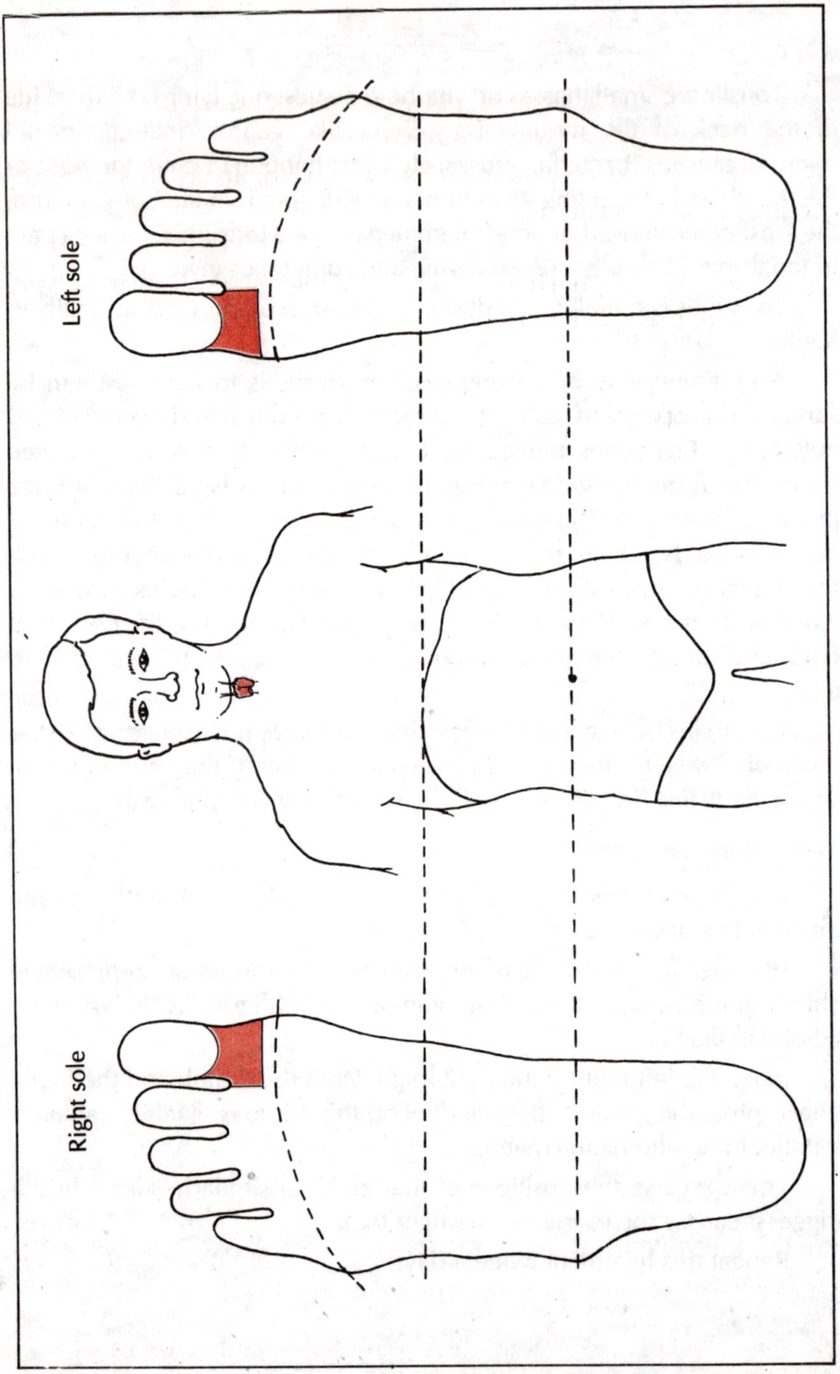

Fig. 7.4

PROBLEMS OF THE LARYNX

Larynx, lying in the neck region, is a tube-like part of the respiratory passage and contains the vocal cords (voice box).

Excessive speaking (or shouting), smoking or an invasion by disease-causing micro-organisms may cause a swelling of the larynx, termed **laryngitis.**

Symptoms of laryngitis include hoarseness or loss of voice, pain in the throat especially while speaking or swallowing and sometimes fever.

Reflex Zone Therapy :

(A) General treatment of the whole body : Start with general treatment as described on page 33.

(B) Specific treatment of the larynx : The larynx is represented at the base of the big toe, as shown in the adjoining diagram.

Using the thumb and the index finger, firmly pinch the base of each big toe, and press in an alternating manner, for about a minute. Repeat this treatment twice a day.

(C) In case of severe pain in the throat, tie small rubber-bands on the two big toes for about 10-12 minutes. During this period, if a toe starts paining or turns black, remove the band for a while (till the normal colour returns) and then reapply it. If necessary, repeat after an hour.

Other measures :

Give your voice complete rest with a view to hastening recovery.

Inhalation of steam for 4-5 minutes, once or twice a day, also helps a lot.

PROBLEMS OF THE LUNGS

Cough; Asthma; Bronchitis; Pleuritis; Pneumonia; Tuberculosis

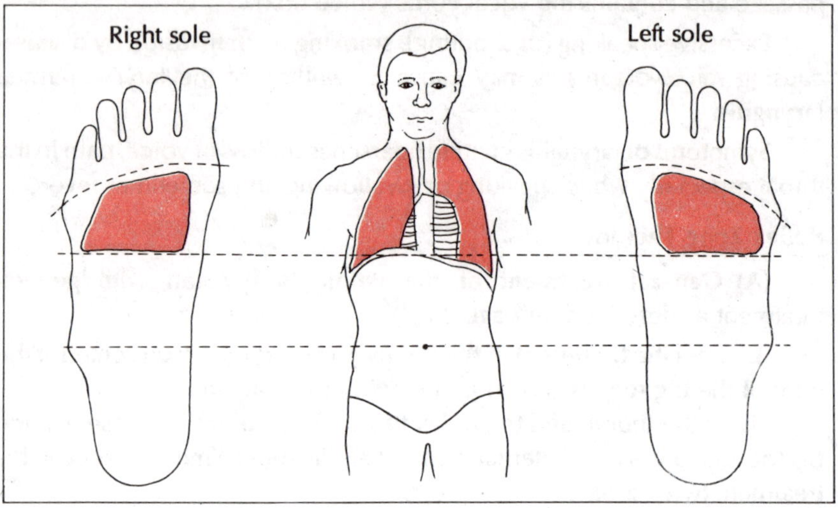

Fig. 7.5

Lungs are the chief respiratory organs, serving to enrich the blood with oxygen, the life-sustaining gas. The blood, then, carries this oxygen to each and every cell of the body.

Asthma is an allergic disorder characterized by breathlessness (dyspnoea), which is the result of a spasmodic narrowing of the respiratory passage.

Bronchitis means an inflammation (swelling) of the bronchi, usually due to an infection.

Pleuritis means an inflammation of the pleura, which is a double-layered protective membrane present around each lung.

Pneumonia means an inflammation of the lung tissue.

Tuberculosis is a specific, communicable, infectious disease of the lungs caused by bacteria 'Mycobacterium tuberculosis'. This serious disease is still widely prevalent in developing countries.

Chief symptoms of lung-disorders include–

(1) Cough, which is nature's method of expelling out any offending matter that is present in the respiratory tract. With cough, the sufferer may bring out sputum, which may be watery or viscous and sometimes

purulent. Since cough is a protective reflex, it is criminal to suppress it with over-the-counter cough syrups.

(2) Breathlessness

(3) Chest pain, made worse by breathing

(4) Sometimes voice problems, sore throat or blood in sputum

Reflex Zone Therapy :

(A) General treatment of the whole body : Start with general treatment as described on page 33.

(B) Specific treatment of the lungs : The lungs are represented on the soles, between the shoulder and the diaphragm lines, as shown in the adjoining diagram. Visualize these trigger areas on your own feet. If necessary, delineate them with a pen.

Now, place the left foot on the right thigh. Steady this foot with the left hand. Start 'walking' your right thumb over the lung area in small steps, taking care not to omit even a smallest spot. While covering the lung area in this manner, every time you encounter a sore spot, stop moving the thumb further and with its tip give deep, alternating pressure for about a minute.

After covering the entire lung area on the left foot, reverse the positions on the legs and in a similar manner stimulate the lung area on the right foot.

Repeat this treatment twice a day.

(C) For relieving an acute attack of asthma, also stimulate the trigger areas for the adrenal glands (see page 89) and tie small rubber-bands on all toes for 10-12 minutes. During this time, if a toe starts paining or turns black, remove the concerned band for a while (till the normal colour returns) and then reapply it.

8. REFLEXOLOGY IN DISORDERS OF THE DIGESTIVE SYSTEM

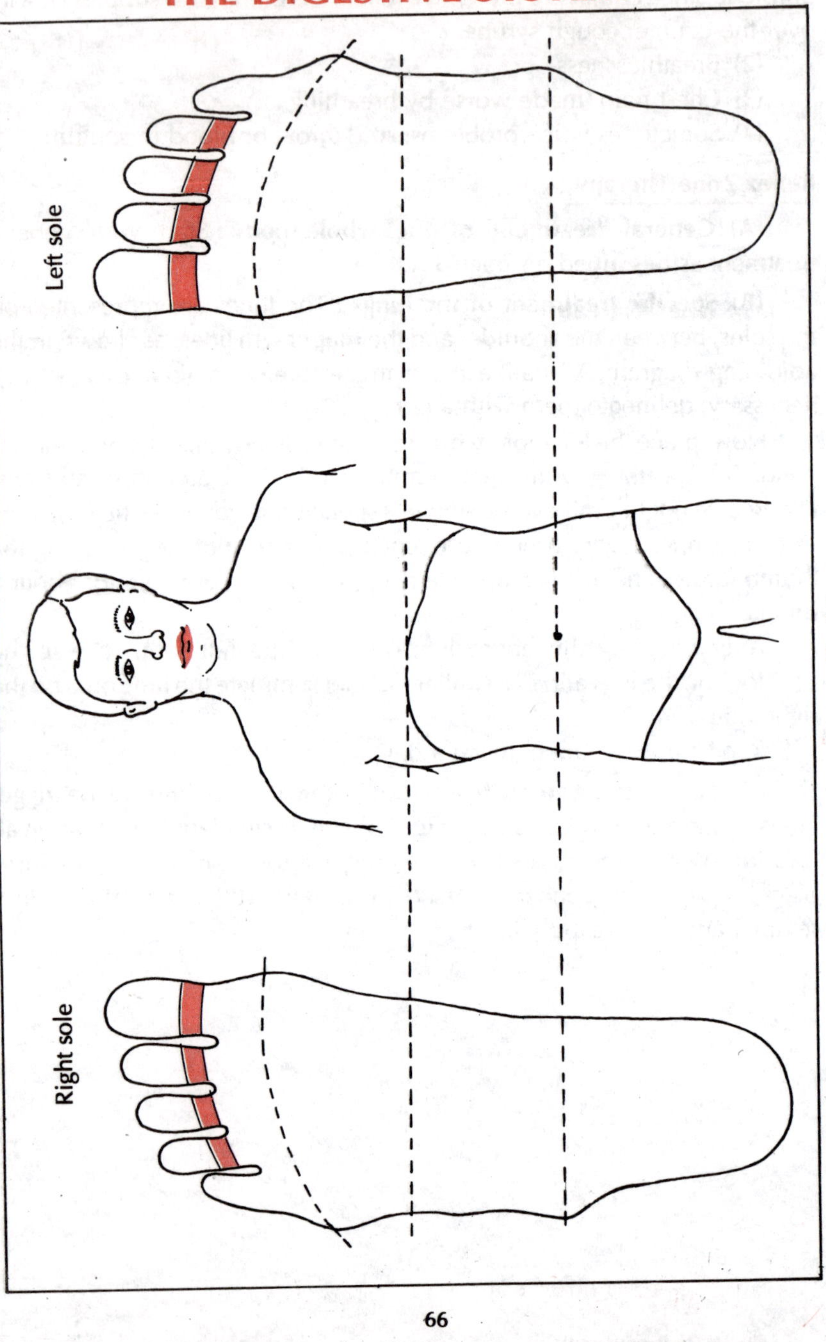

Fig. 8.1

PROBLEMS OF THE MOUTH

Excessive salivation; Aphthous ulcers; Gingivitis; Glossitis

Tiny, white ulcers on the inner surfaces of the lips or the cheeks are called **aphthous ulcers.**

Gingivitis is an inflammation (swelling) of the gums.

Glossitis is an inflammation (swelling) of the tongue.

Reflex Zone Therapy :

(A) General treatment of the whole body : Start with general treatment as described on page 33.

(B) Specific treatment of the mouth : The mouth is represented on the first four toes as shown in the adjoining diagram.

With the help of the thumb and the first finger, pinch each of the eight toes for about one minute, giving pressure in an alternating manner.

Repeat this treatment twice a day.

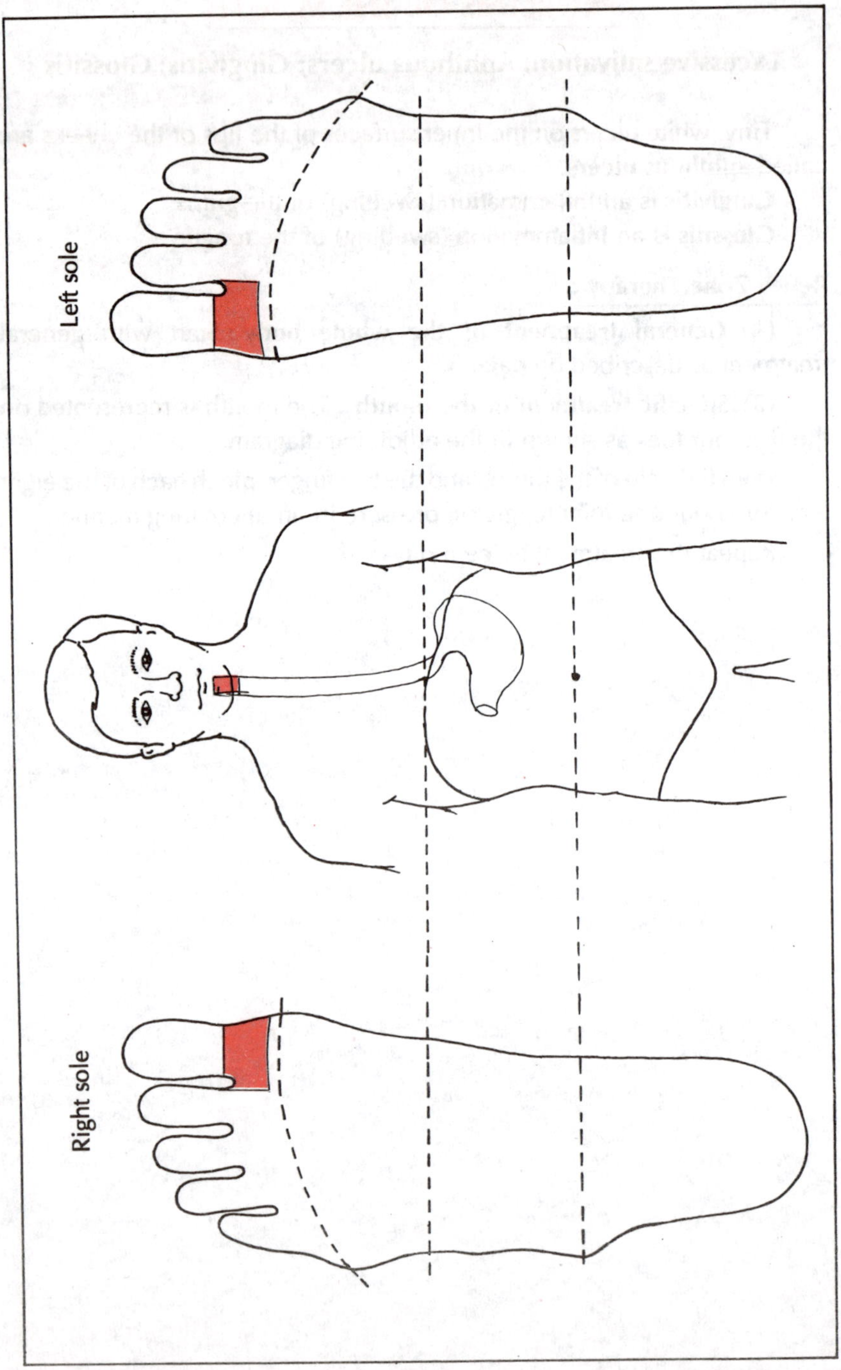

Fig. 8.2

PROBLEMS OF THE THROAT

Sore throat (pharyngitis); difficulty in swallowing

Sometimes, an infection of the upper respiratory tract (e.g., common cold) spreads down to cause **sore throat.**

The most initial symptoms include a tickling sensation in the throat and a feeling of rawness. These are then replaced by real pain in the throat and **difficulty in swallowing (dysphagia).** In severe cases, other symptoms like general malaise, fever and tenderness of lymph nodes below the lower jaw may be present.

Reflex Zone Therapy :

(A) General treatment of the whole body : Start with general treatment as described on page 33.

(B) Specific treatment of the throat : The throat is represented at the base of the two big toes as shown in the adjoining diagram.

Place the thumb on the upper surface and the index finger on the lower surface of the left big toe and give deep alternating pressure for about a minute. Similarly, press upon the trigger area for the throat on the right big toe.

Repeat this treatment twice a day.

(C) For very severe pain : Tie small rubber-bands on the two big toes for about 10-12 minutes. During this time, if a toe starts paining or turns black, remove the band for a while (till the normal colour returns) and then reapply it. If necessary, repeat after an hour.

Other treatment : Gargling with warm salt-water 3-4 times a day proves very helpful.

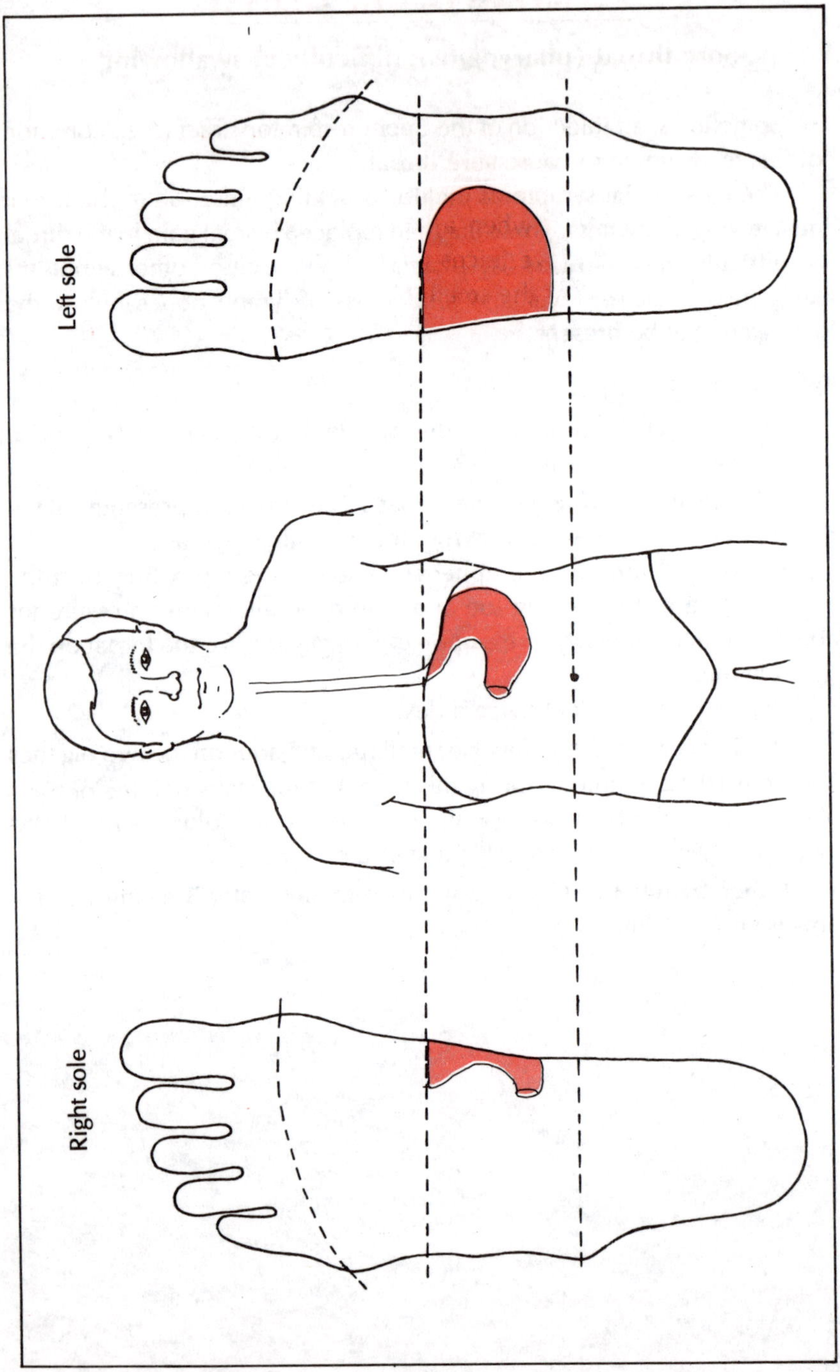

Fig. 8.3

PROBLEMS OF THE STOMACH

Gastritis; Burning/ Ulcer in the Stomach; Indigestion

Gastritis means an inflammation (swelling) of the inner surface of the stomach. Symptoms of gastritis are nausea, vomiting and burning pain in the stomach.

An ulcer is formed when a small spot on the stomach wall gets dissolved by the digestive juices (acid-pepsin). Similar ulceration may occur in the first part of the small intestine (duodenum). In both types, there is a long-standing history of pain in the pit of the stomach. Pain is so well defined as can be shown by the tip of a finger. Features that help in differentiating between a **stomach (gastric) ulcer** and an intestinal (duodenal) ulcer have been tabulated below :

Gastric ulcer	Duodenal ulcer
Pain increases on taking food. Therefore, the victim abstains from food and gradually loses weight. Pain typically occurs within an hour after a meal.	Pain lessens on taking food. Therefore, the victim frequently takes food and gradually puts on weight. Pain typically occurs between two meals. Many persons complain of midnight (12 to 2 am) pain.

Reflex Zone Therapy :

(A) General treatment of the whole body : Start with general treatment as described on page 33.

(B) Specific treatment of the stomach : The stomach is represented on the two soles as shown in the adjoining diagram. Visualize these trigger areas on your own feet. If necessary, delineate them with a pen.

Now, place the left foot on the right thigh. Steady this foot with the left hand. Start 'walking' the right thumb over the 'stomach area' in small steps taking care not to omit even a smallest spot. During such probing, every time you encounter a sore spot, stop moving the thumb further and with its tip give deep, alternating pressure for a minute.

After covering the entire stomach area on the left sole, reverse the positions of the legs and stimulate the trigger area for the stomach on the right sole.

Repeat this treatment twice a day.

(C) Pinching the web (skin) between the big toe and the second toes for 1-2 minutes, 2-3 times a day, has also helped many persons.

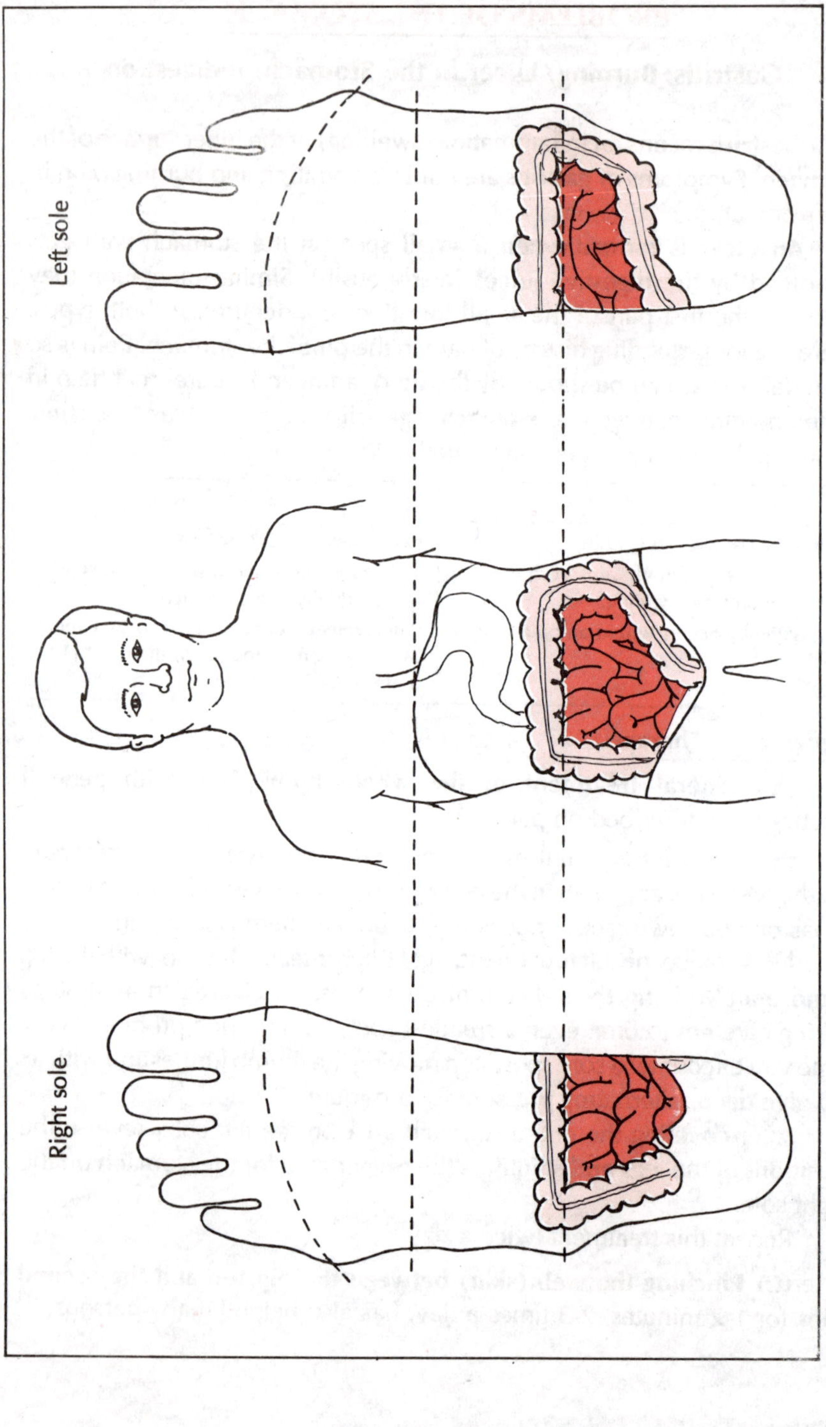

Fig. 8.4

PROBLEMS OF THE INTESTINES

Duodenal ulcer; Constipation; Flatulence (gas); Diarrhoea (loose motions); Dysentery; Colitis

More than 20 feet long small intestine and about 5 feet long large intestine together occupy most of the space in the abdomen.

A small ulcer formed in the first part of the small intestine is called a **duodenal ulcer.** For characteristic features see 'Problems of the stomach' (pg. 71).

Colitis means an inflammation (swelling) of the large intestine.

Diarrhoea means frequent passage of loose stools. Severe diarrhoea may lead to dehydration.

Constipation is the reverse condition of diarrhoea. Stools are not passed at the expected time. When stools remain for a long time in the large intestine, they turn hard and require force for explusion.

Stools that stagnate in the large intestine undergo decomposition. This produces **gases (flatulence).**

Dysentery is a disease characterised by abdominal pain and frequent ill-formed stools with mucous and blood. It is caused by an infection with bacteria or amoebae.

Reflex Zone Therapy :

(A) General treatment of the whole body : Start with general treatment as described on page 33.

(B) Specific treatment of the intestines : The intestines are represented on both soles as shown in the adjoining diagram. Visualize these trigger areas on your own feet. If necessary, delineate them with a pen.

Now, place the left foot on the right thigh. Steady this foot with the left hand. Start 'walking' the right thumb over the 'intestinal area' in small steps, taking care not to omit even a smallest spot. During such probing, every time you encounter a sore spot, stop moving the thumb further and with its tip give deep, alternating pressure for about a minute.

After covering the entire intestinal area on the left sole, reverse the positions of the legs and in a similar manner, stimulate the trigger area for the intestines on the right sole.

Repeat this treatment twice a day.

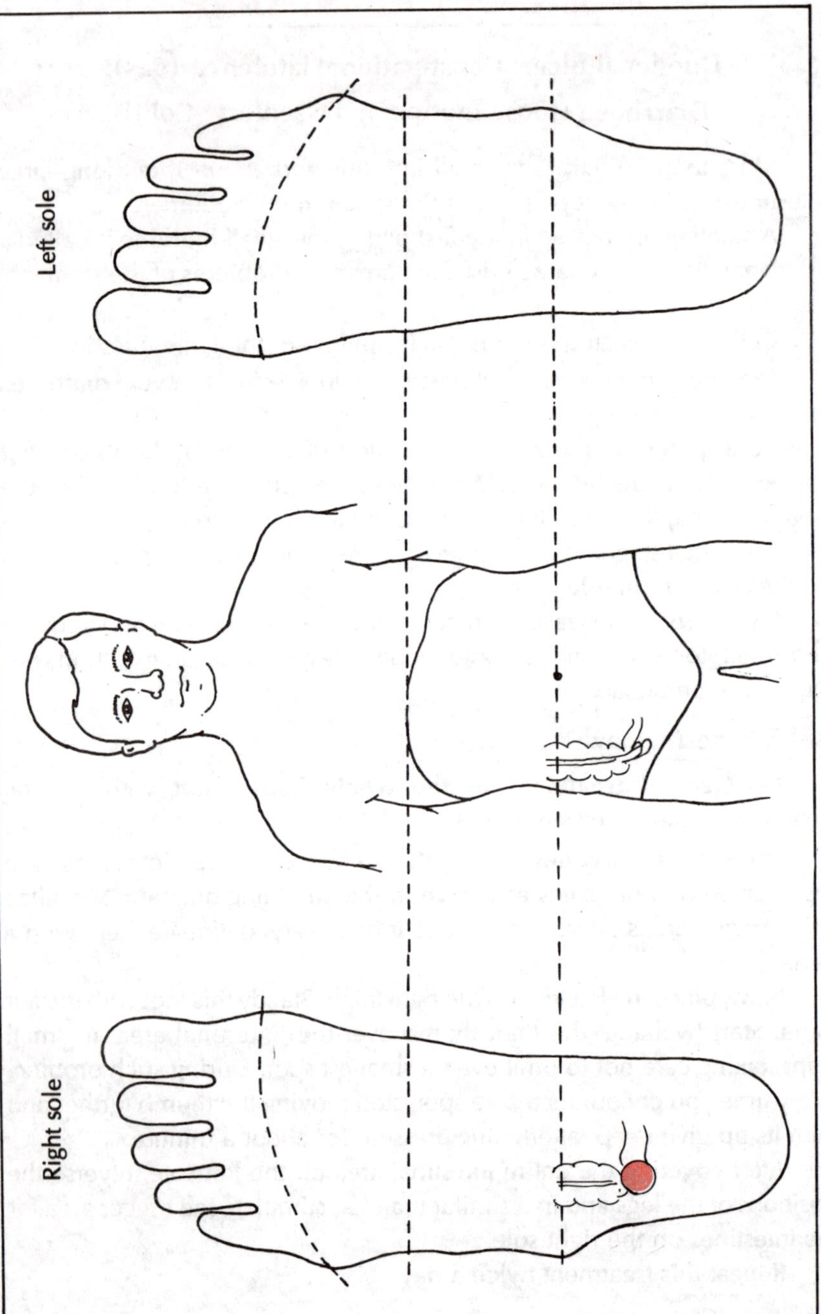

Fig. 8.5

PROBLEMS OF THE APPENDIX

Appendicitis

Appendix is a small, finger-like organ present at the junction of the small and the large intestines. In grass-eating animals, it is very well developed and works to digest cellulose. However, in human beings,it is vestigeal (non-functional).

An inflammation (swelling) of the appendix is called **appendicitis.** It is believed that the rapid rise in the incidence of appendicitis in recent years is the consequence of modernization : highly refined, soft, low roughage diet and sedentary life.

Symptoms of appendicitis include : (1) sudden onset of abdominal pain, initially felt near the navel but ultimately shifting to the right groin, (2) nausea, sometimes followed by vomiting, (3) foul breath, (4) general malaise and fever.

Putting forth the argument that a swollen appendix may burst into the abdomen causing grave complications, surgeons usually remove the appendix. In medical circles, it is jokingly said that Appendicectomy is to a general surgeon what tonsillectomy is to a ENT surgeon : bread and butter.

Reflex Zone Therapy :

(A) General treatment of the whole body : Start with general treatment as described on page 33.

(B) Specific treatment of the appendix : As shown in the adjoining diagram, the trigger spot for the appendix is located on the right sole, just near the heel.

Place the right foot on the left thigh. On deep probing of the concerned area of the sole, you will be able to determine a sore spot, corresponding with the appendix. With the thumb-tip, give deep, alternating pressure on this spot for about two minutes.

Repeat this treatment twice a day.

(C) For very severe pain, tie small rubber-bands on the 4th and the 5th toes of the right foot for 10-12 minutes. During this period,if a toe starts aching or turns black, remove the concerned band for a while (till the normal colour returns) and then reapply it. If necessary, repeat after an hour.

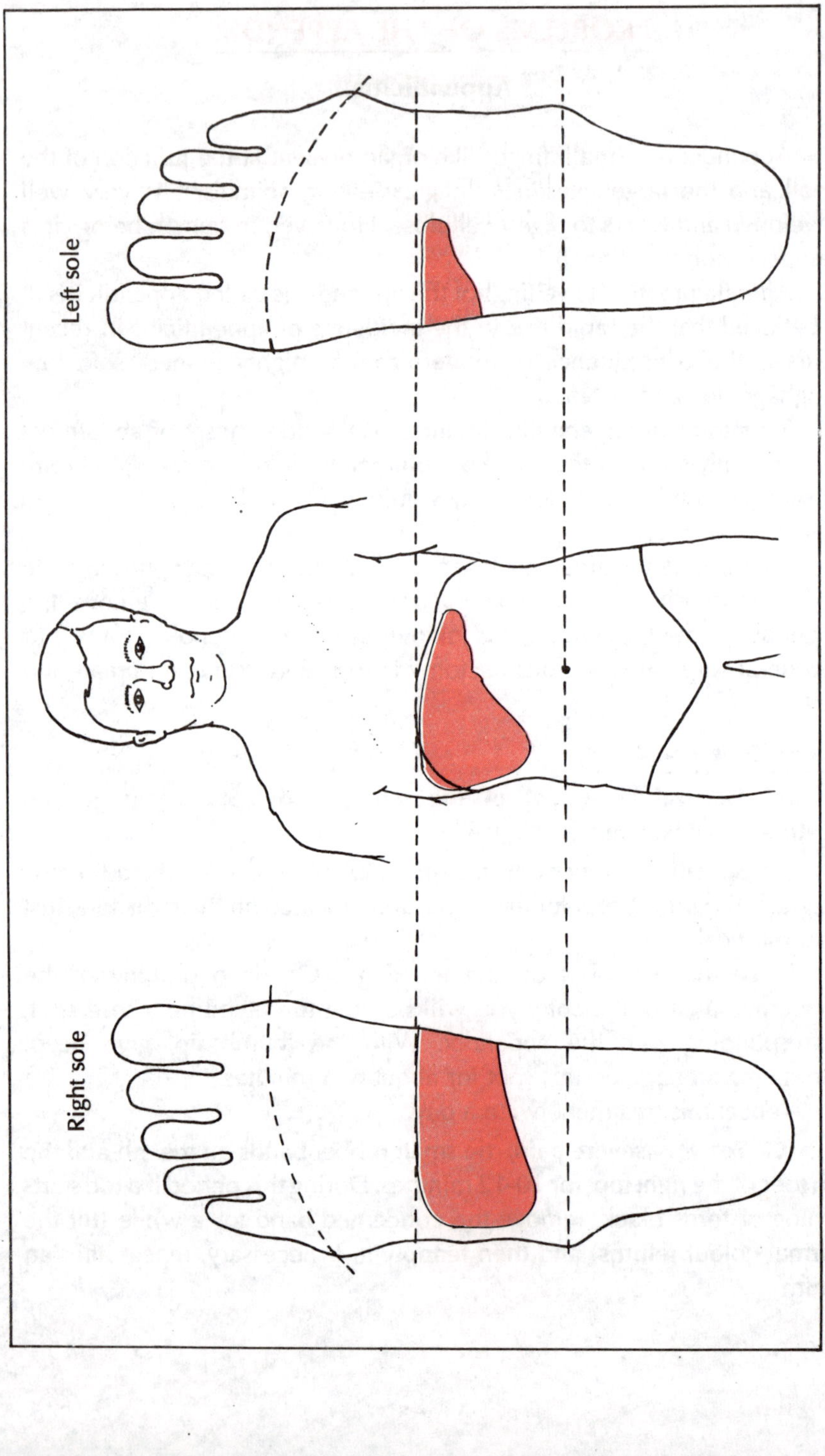

Fig. 8.6

PROBLEMS OF THE LIVER

Jaundice; Hepatitis

Liver is the largest organ of the body weighing about $1\frac{1}{2}$ kg. It is a gigantic, multipurpose chemical factory which carries out a host of activities, notable among which are detoxification of the blood and production of an important digestive juice called the bile.

Had it not been for the liver, it would be impossible for us to consume substances like alcohol and deadly chemicals (in the form of medicines) with impunity.

The most common disease of liver dysfunction is **jaundice,** characterized by a yellow discoloration of the skin, nails, eyes, mucous membranes and excretions. Other symptoms include nausea, vomiting, loss of appetite and extreme fatigue. Jaundice is usually caused either by a viral infection of the liver (viral hepatitis) or an obstruction to the flow of bile.

Alcohol acts as a poison on the liver. Prolonged consumption of large quantities of alcohol damages the liver and gives rise to a grave condition called **cirrhosis.**

Despite vociferous claims to the contrary, medicinal treatment for jaundice is, at best, palliative or supportive.

Reflex Zone Therapy :

(A) General treatment of the whole body : Start with general treatment as described on page 33.

(B) Specific treatment of the liver : The liver is represented on both soles as shown in the adjoining diagram. Visualize the 'liver area' on your own feet. If necessary, delineate it with a pen.

Now, place the left foot on the right thigh. Steady this foot with the left hand. Now, start 'walking' the thumb over the liver area, in small steps, taking care not to omit even a smallest spot. During such probing, every time you encounter a sore spot, stop moving the thumb further and with its tip, give deep, alternating pressure for about a minute.

After covering the entire liver area on the left sole, reverse the positions of the legs and in a similar manner, stimulate the trigger area for the liver on the right sole.

Repeat this treatment twice a day.

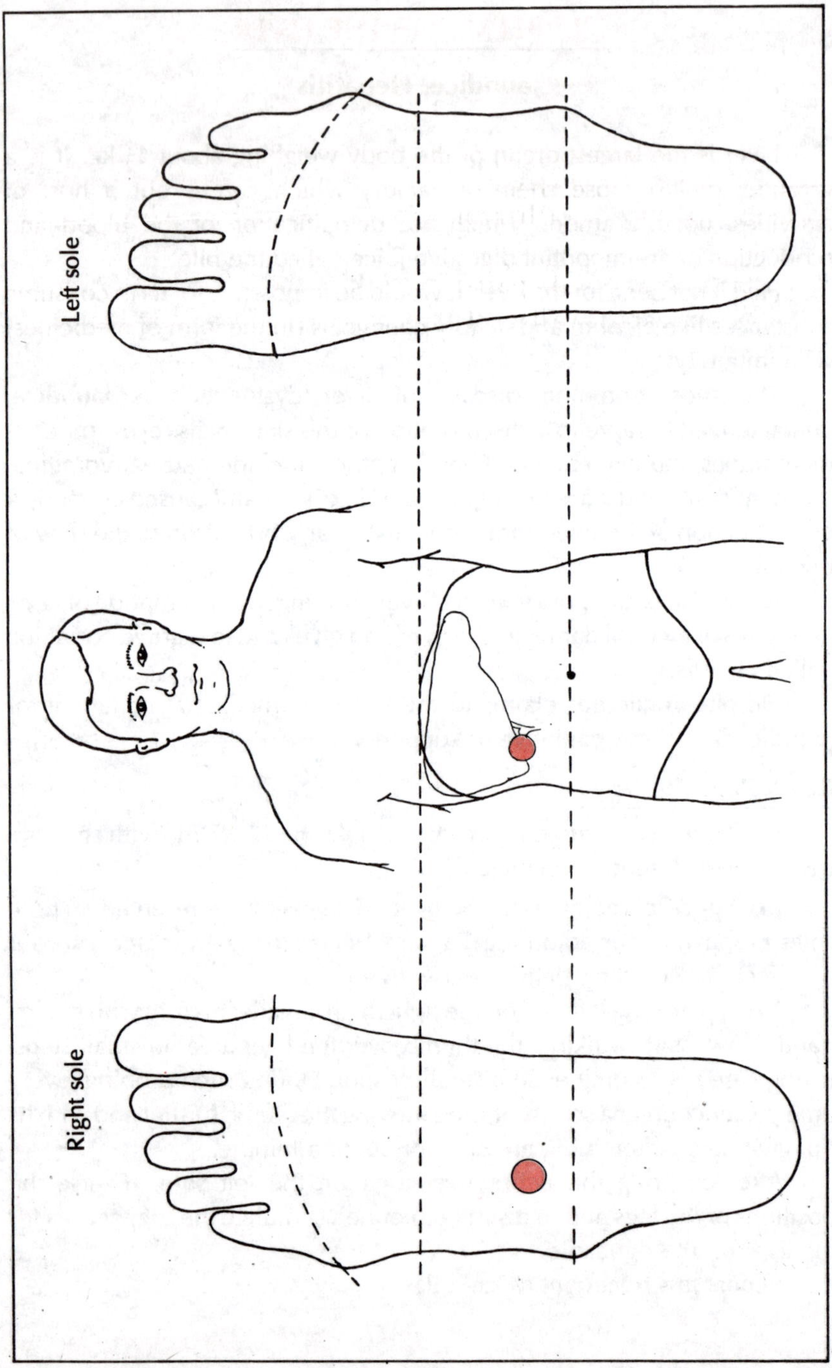

Fig. 8.7

PROBLEMS OF THE GALL BLADDER

Gall stone; Cholecystitis

Liver produces the digestive juice 'bile' all the time. However, this bile is not needed in the digestive tract all the time. It is required sometime after food is consumed. Till then, bile is stored and concentrated in the gall bladder.

Gall bladder is a small pear-shaped organ situated below the liver.

An inflammation (swelling) of the gall bladder is termed **cholecystitis.**

Gall bladder may also develop **stones** in its cavity.

Symptoms of gall bladder disease include nausea, belching, a sensation of fullness in the stomach and sometimes severe pain in the abdomen (**gall colic**).

Reflex Zone Therapy :

(A) General treatment of the whole body : Start with general treatment as described on page 33.

(B) Specific treatment of the gall bladder : The gall bladder is represented on the right sole just above the navel line as shown in the adjoining diagram.

Place the right foot on the left thigh. On deep probing of the concerned area of the sole, you will be able to locate a sore spot, corresponding with the gall bladder. With the thumb-tip, give deep, alternating pressure on this spot for about two minutes.

Repeat this treatment twice a day.

(C) In case of gall colic : Tie small rubber-bands on the 4th and 5th toes of the right foot for 10-12 minutes. During this period, if a toe starts paining or turns black, remove the concerned band for a while (till the normal colour returns) and then reapply it. If necessary, repeat after an hour.

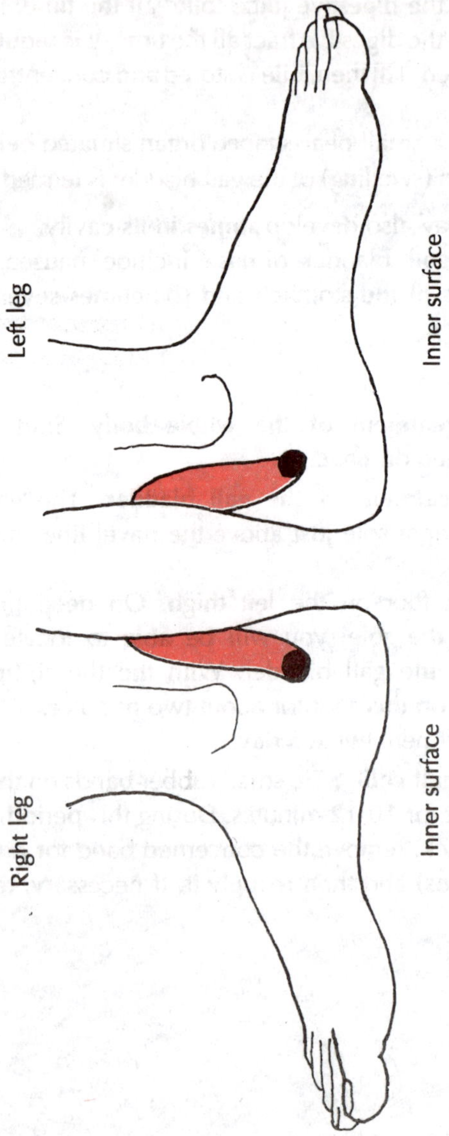

Fig. 8.8

PROBLEMS OF THE ANUS

Piles (haemorrhoids); Anal fissure; Anal fistula

Problems of the anus are not only painful but also extremely embarrassing. More often than not, they are the end-results of constipation – the scourge of modern life.

All of us have seen swollen, tortuous, bluish veins on the calves of some people. These are varicosed veins. **Piles** is a varicosed condition of the veins of the anus. These produce a lot of pain and, sometimes, bleed profusely.

Anal fissure is a painful linear ulcer (crack) at the anus.

Anal fistula is an abnormal extra channel that is created between the rectum and the skin around the anus. Symptoms of anal fistula include pain and discharge of pus (or blood) through the abnormal opening, soiling the clothes.

Reflex Zone Therapy :

(A) General treatment of the whole body : Start with general treatment as described on page 33.

(B) Specific treatment of the anus : Together, the anus, the anal canal and the rectum are represented on the inner surfaces of the two feet, in the form of longitudinal bands (see the adjoining diagram).

Place the left foot on the right thigh. Starting from the inner surface of the heel, 'walk' the right thumb upward along the trigger band for anus, in small steps, taking care not to omit even a smallest spot. During such probing, every time you come across a sore spot, stop moving the thumb further and with its tip, give deep, alternating pressure for about a minute.

After covering the entire 'anus area' on the left foot, interchange the positions of the legs and in a similar manner stimulate the trigger area for the anus on the right foot.

9. REFLEXOLOGY IN DISORDERS OF THE CARDIO-VASCULAR SYSTEM

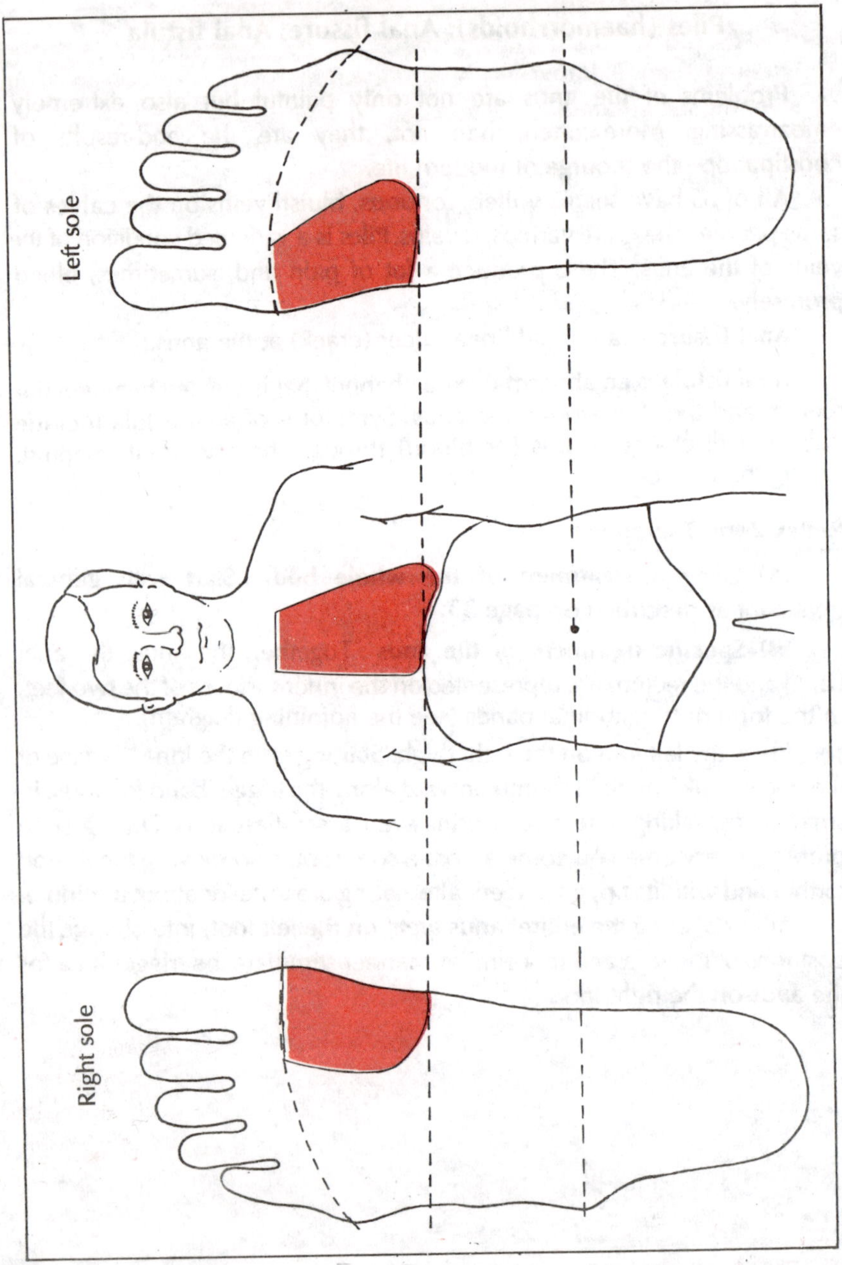

Fig. 9.1

PROBLEMS OF THE HEART

Palpitations; Angina pectoris

Heart is an extraordinary natural pump that is responsible for maintaining the circulation of blood in the body.

On an average, it beats (contracts) 72 times a minute. With each beat, it pumps about 70 ml of blood into the arteries. Thus, during the day, it pushes almost 72,59,000 ml of blood into the circulation, an incredible feat considering the fact that it is very small (about the size of a closed fist), weighs only 250-300 gms and works ceaselessly or tirelessly, never thinking of a break or a vacation.

The heart beats so silently that we are normally unaware of its working. Sometimes, however, it contracts so violently that the person is able to feel and/or hear its beats. This condition is called **palpitations.** Usually, palpitations are not a symptom of a disease but merely a result of physical exercise or emotional excitement.

The heart, which nourishes each and every cell of the body through blood, depends for its own nourishment on the two coronary arteries. If these are partially blocked (say by cholesterol), the heart cannot receive adequate nourishment. This causes chest-pain termed **angina pectoris.** Angina pain is precipitated by physical exercise (when heart needs extra blood) and is relieved by rest. The condition, if not treated adequately, may ultimately culminate into a heart attack.

Reflex Zone Therapy :

(A) General treatment of the whole body : Start with general treatment as described on page 33.

(B) Specific treatment of the heart : The heart is represented on both the soles, between the shoulder line and the diaphragm line as shown in the adjoining diagram. Visualize these areas on your own feet. If necessary, delineate them with a pen.

Now, place the left foot on the right thigh and steady it with the left hand. Start 'walking your right' thumb over the heart area in small steps, taking care not to omit even a smallest spot. During such probing, every time you encounter a sore spot, stop moving the thumb further and with its tip give deep, alternating pressure for about a minute.

After covering the entire 'heart area' on the left foot, reverse the positions of the legs and in a similar manner stimulate the trigger area for the heart on the right foot.

Repeat this treatment twice a day.

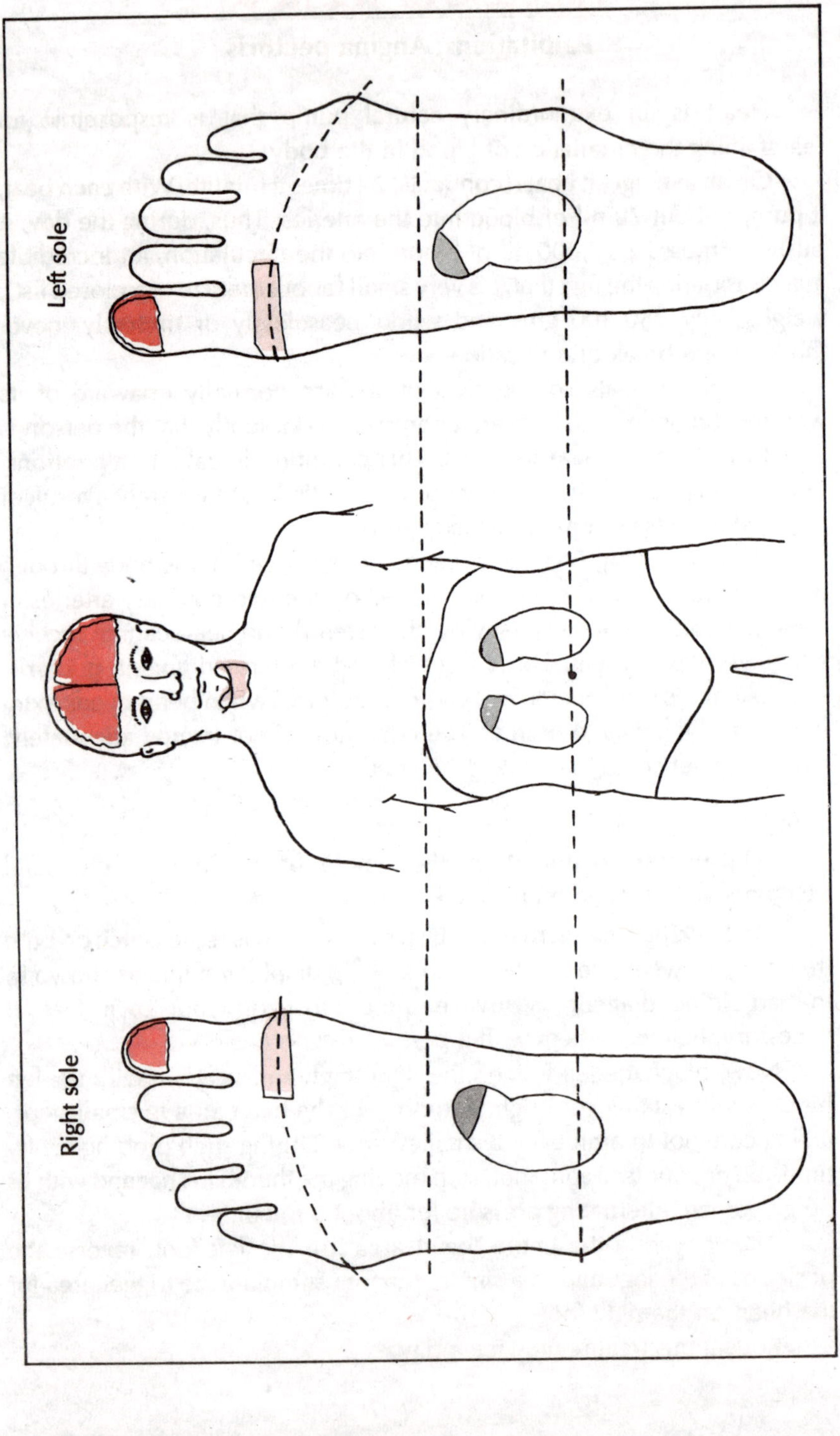

Fig. 9.2

HIGH BLOOD PRESSURE (HYPERTENSION); LOW BLOOD PRESSURE

Blood pressure is simply the pressure exerted by the circulating blood on the walls of blood-vessels.

When the heart contracts, it forcefully drives the blood into the arteries. The pressure at such a time is more and is termed systolic blood pressure. When the heart relaxes, the pressure is relatively less and is termed diastolic blood pressure. A systolic BP of 120 mm Hg and a diastolic BP of 80 mm Hg are considered normal. These pressures are denoted as 120/80. The body tries to maintain blood pressure within a narrow range, allowing it neither to rise nor fall. This mechanism, called homoeostasis, is necessary for the well-being of a person.

A persistent rise of blood pressure above the level of 150/90 mm Hg, recorded on three or more successive occasions is defined as **high blood pressure.**

It is fallaciously believed that high BP causes headaches, redness of eyes or the face, swelling of neck-veins etc. The fact is : it gives rise to no symptoms. If not adequately controlled, it ruins the various organs of the body, causing grave complications. Therefore, it is called a 'silent killer'.

On the other hand, **low blood pressure** is a harmless condition. Renowned experts and authorities on the heart have unanimously opined that persons with low BP may experience mild fatigue at the end of the day or occasional bouts of transitory dizziness; but they go on to live for 120 years !

Reflex Zone Therapy :

(A) General treatment of the whole body : Start with general treatment as described on page 33.

(B) Specific stimulation of trigger areas of the following :

– **Mind/Brain** (including pituitary gland and hypothalamus, the seat of autonomous nervous system)

– **Thyroid gland**

– **Adrenal gland**

Slowly walk your thumb over trigger areas for the above mentioned organs in small steps, taking care not to omit even a smallest spot. During such probing, every time you come across sore spot, stop moving the thumb further and with its tip, give deep, alternating pressure for about a minute.

Repeat this treatment twice a day.

10. REFLEXOLOGY IN DISORDERS OF THE EXCRETORY SYSTEM

PROBLEMS OF THE KIDNEYS

Inflammation of renal tissue; Kidney failure; Kidney stone

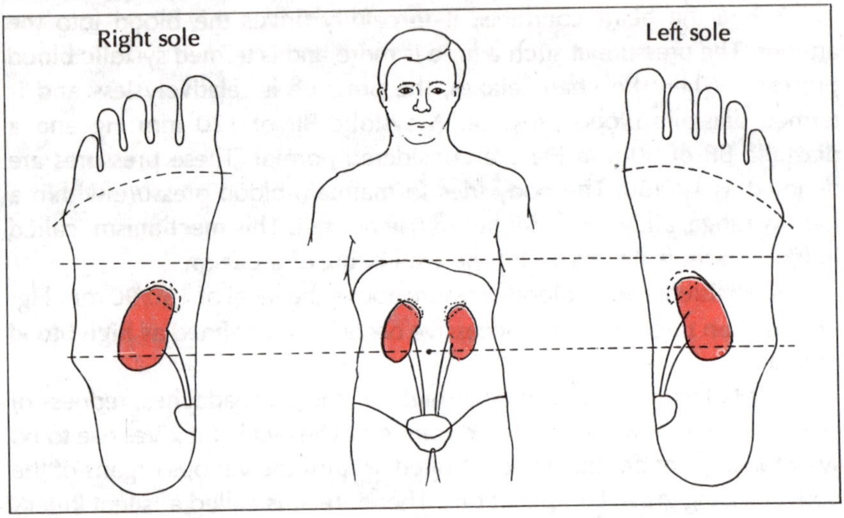

Fig. 10.1

Kidneys are the chief excretory organs of the body. They are extremely efficient natural filters that purify blood by removing from it waste products of metabolism like urea, uric acid and creatinine.

Twice the total quantity of blood present in our body passes through and gets filtered by the two kidneys every hour. In the process about $1\frac{1}{2}$ litre of urine is formed every 24 hours. Moreover, kidneys help in regulating blood pressure, producing red blood cells and controlling the quantities of salts and water in the blood.

Occasionally, kidneys fall victims to infectious or auto-immune disorders, leading to their inflammation (**nephritis**) and causing symptoms like pain in the loins (which radiates forward into the penis or the scrotum), discoloured (milky or bloody) and foul smelling urine and disturbances of BP.

If a kidney-disease is not adequately treated, kidney-tissue may undergo destruction causing **renal failure.** This leads to uremia (accumulation of metabolic wastes in the blood) which is characterized by nausea, vomiting, lethargy, drowsiness or even death. Renal failure may also be a complication of other diseases like diabetes or high BP. A person with renal failure requires **dialysis**–by which blood is artificially filtered.

Sometimes, a **stone** develops in one of the kidneys. If it obstructs the flow of urine, it may cause severe pain in the loins. A stone is clearly visualized on an X-ray picture.

Reflex Zone Therapy :

(A) General treatment of the whole body : Start with general treatment as described on page 33.

(B) Specific treatment of the kidneys : The right and the left kidneys are represented on the right and the left soles respectively as shown in the adjoining figure.

Even if only one kidney has a disorder, it is advisable to stimulate trigger areas on both the feet. Visualize the kidney areas on the two feet. If necessary, delineate them with a pen.

Now, place the left foot on the right thigh. Steady this foot with the left hand. Start 'walking' the right thumb over the kidney area on the left sole in small steps, taking care not to omit even a smallest spot. During such probing, every time you come across a sore spot, stop moving the thumb further and with its tip give deep, alternating pressure for about a minute.

After covering the entire kidney area on the left foot, reverse the positions of the legs and in a similar manner stimulate the trigger area for the right kidney on the right foot.

Repeat this treatment twice a day.

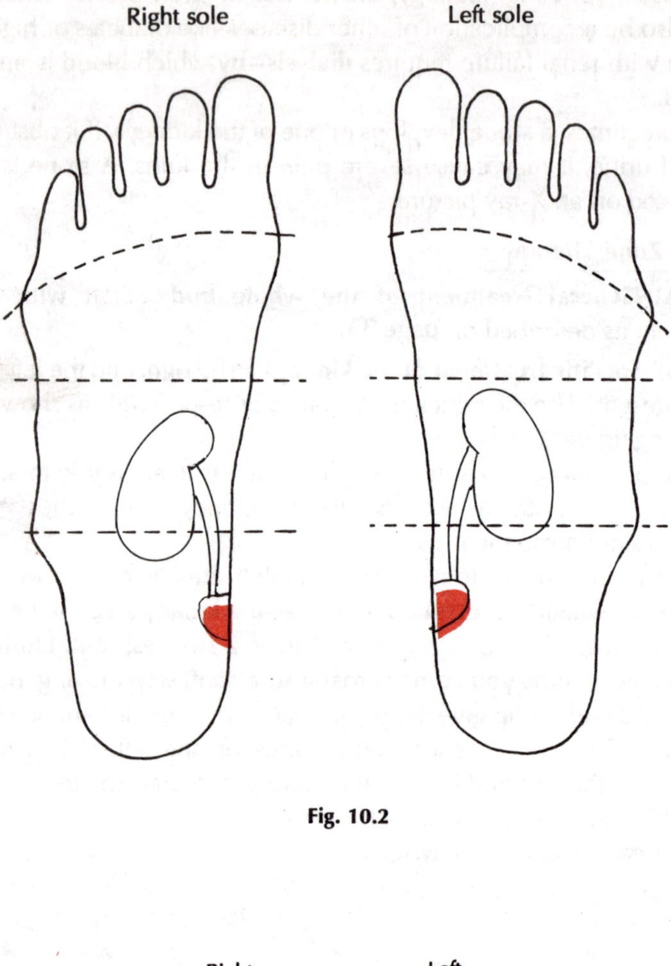

Fig. 10.2

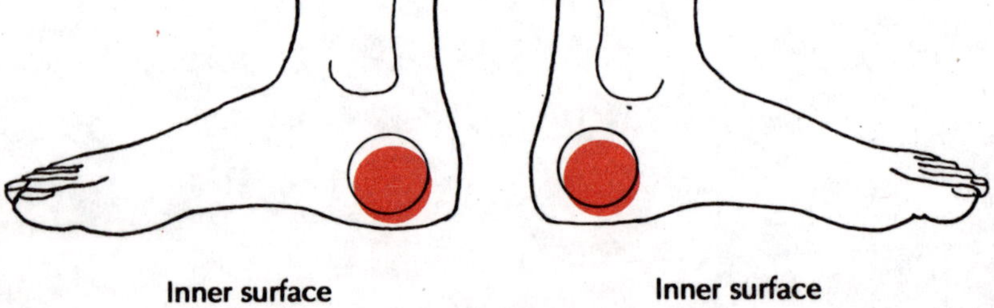

Fig. 10.3

PROBLEMS OF THE URINARY BLADDER AND URETHRA

Cystitis; Urethritis; Bed-wetting in Children

The kidneys constantly filter blood and form urine. This trickles along the ureters to reach the urinary bladder, where it starts accumulating. When the bladder gets full, there is a desire to pass urine. Then, the band-like sphincter muscle at the bottom of the bladder is let loose and urine passes through the urethra to reach the exterior.

Inflammations of the urinary bladder and the urethra are termed **cystitis** and **urethritis** respectively. Women suffer from these problems more frequently than men. Symptoms include : pain in the lower abdomen just above the genitals, burning sensation while or after passing urine, desire to pass more urine even after the bladder has been emptied, cloudy and/or foul-smelling urine, etc.

Another problem associated with the bladder is **bed-wetting in children.** A child loses control over its bladder and passes urine in the bed at night, Usually, no obvious cause can be detected for this problem.

Reflex Zone Therapy :

(A) General treatment of the whole body : Start with general treatment as described on page 33.

(B) Specific treatment of the bladder : The urinary bladder is represented less on the sole but more on the medial (inner) aspect of the heel, as shown in the adjoining figure.

Place the left foot on the right thigh. Steady this foot with the left hand. Now, with the tip of the right thumb, give deep, alternating pressure, first on the sole part and then on the heel part of the bladder area, for about a minute each.

Next, reverse the positions of the legs and in a similar manner stimulate the trigger areas for the bladder on the right foot.

Repeat this treatment twice a day.

11. REFLEXOLOGY IN DISORDERS OF THE REPRODUCTIVE SYSTEM

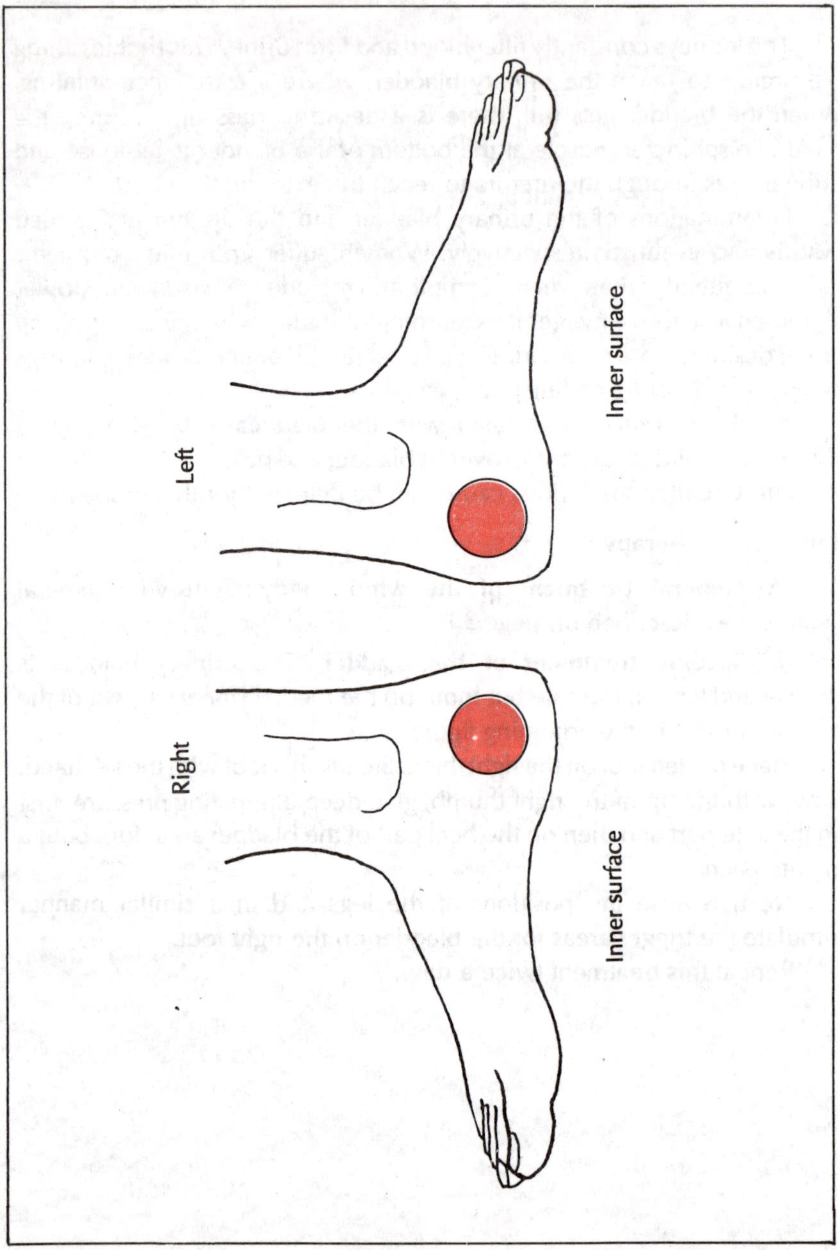

Fig. 11.1

PROBLEMS OF MEN

Hydrocele; Varicocele; Enlarged prostate; Impotence; Oligospermia

Hydrocele is a collection of fluid in the layers of tissue surrounding the testicle. It is characterized by a swelling in the scrotum which is not painful but only uncomfortable.

Varicocele is the varicosed condition of veins in the spermatic cord, forming a scrotal swelling that feels like a 'bag of worms'. Varicocele is usually harmless.

Prostatic enlargement is a common disorder of elderly males. Prostate is a plum-sized gland that surrounds the first part of the urethra. An enlarged prostate may press upon the urethra to cause (a) an obstruction to the flow of urine which comes out drop-wise, (b) retention of some urine in the bladder due to which there is a constant urge to urinate, (c) sometimes, burning or pain while passing urine.

Impotence means absent or deficient erection of the penis when attempting sexual intercourse. It is mostly psychological, a result of anxiety. The problem is so distressing that victims run helter-skelter for medical help and fall a prey to unscrupulous quacks.

Oligospermia means a low count of sperms in the semen, making it difficult for a male to fertilize a female.

Reflex Zone Therapy :

(A) General treatment of the whole body : Start with general treatment as described on page 33.

(B) Specific treatment of the genital organs : The genital organs (the penis, the testicles, the prostate) are located on the inner sides of the two heels (see the adjoining diagram).

With the tip of the thumb, press first on the medial side of the left heel and then on the medial side of the right heel, for about a minute each.

Repeat this treatment twice a day.

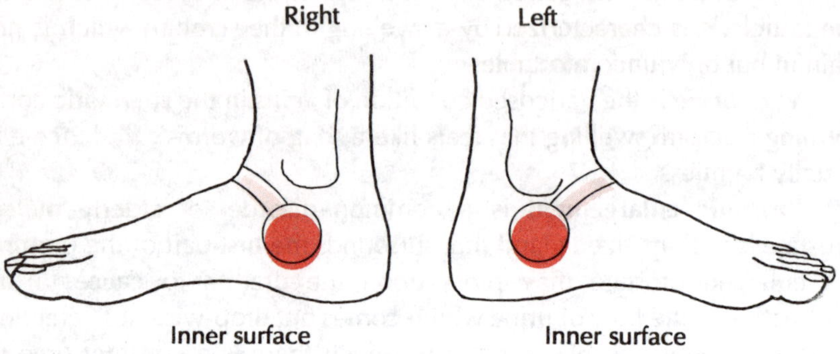

Fig. 11.2

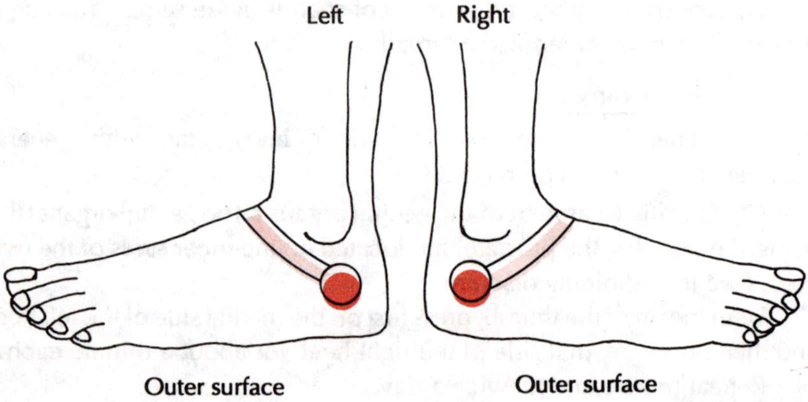

Fig. 11.3

PROBLEMS OF WOMEN

Menstrual disorders; Leucorrhoea

Menstrual disorders and **leucorrhoea (white discharge)** are common problems of women. However, out of a feeling of shame and embarrassment many women do not disclose their problems and continue to suffer silently.

Dysmenorrhoea means 'painful menses'. During the days of menstrual flow, there is pain in abdomen, back, thighs and breasts. Moreover, there may be muscular cramps, headaches, general lassitude and easy irritability. If similar but less severe symptoms appear immediately before the menses, the condition is called pre-menstrual syndrome.

Normally, menses flow about 11 to 13 times in a year. If the frequency is less, the condition is called **oligomenorrhoea.**

Menorrhagia means excessive bleeding during menses.

Leucorrhoea is a common feminine disorder characterized by a discharge of thick white fluid between (usually just before and after) menses. Discharge of only a small quantity of white fluid may be considered normal, but flow of excessive and foul-smelling fluid is a sign of an infection of vagina and/or uterus by fungi.

Reflex Zone Therapy :

(A) General treatment of the whole body : Start with general treatment as described on page 33.

(B) Specific treatment of the genital organs : The genital organs of a woman are represented on the foot in the form of a band around the front aspect of the ankle (see the adjoining diagram).

Place the left foot on the right thigh. Start 'walking' the right thumb along the trigger band in small steps, taking care not to omit even a smallest spot. During such probing, every time you encounter a sore spot, stop moving the thumb further and with its tip give deep, alternating pressure for about a minute.

Next, reverse the positions of the legs and with the left thumb stimulate the trigger areas for the genital organs on the right foot.

Repeat this treatment twice a day.

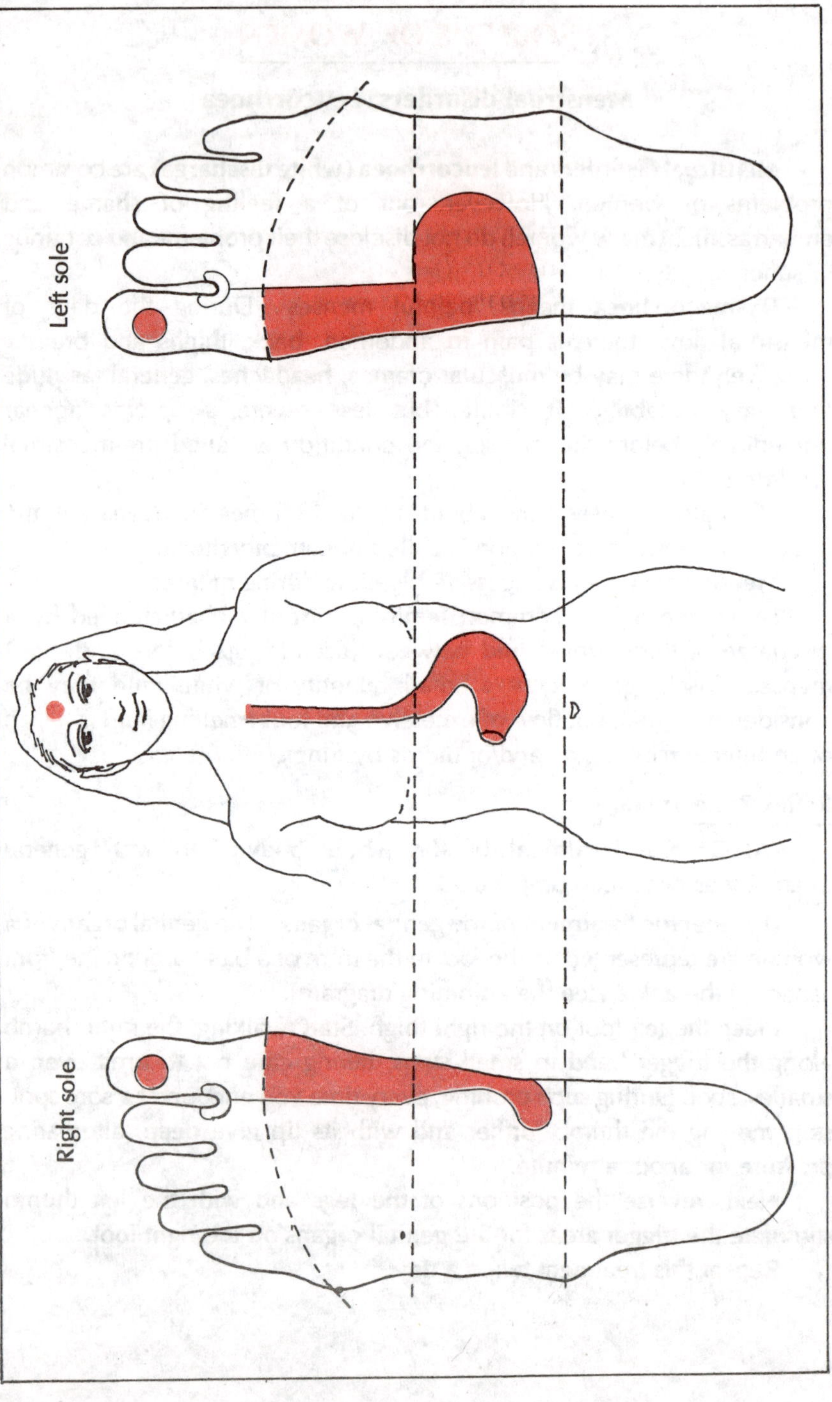

Fig. 11.4

Morning sickness (vomiting during pregnancy)

Occasional, slight vomiting in the morning is a common problem of early pregnancy. This, usually, does no harm and subsides on its own by the end of the third month of pregnancy. Sometimes, however, it extends even into the second trimester of pregnancy and/or assumes a severer form thereby undermining health.

Causes of vomiting during early pregnancy are not clearly understood. Marked hormonal and metabolic changes are considered to be responsible for this.

Reflex Zone Therapy can go a long way towards alleviating this problem.

Reflex Zone Therapy :

(A) General treatment of the whole body : Start with general treatment as described on page 33.

(B) Specific treatment of the pituitary, the oesophagus and the stomach : With your thumb-tip give deep, alternating pressure on the centre of each big toe for about a minute.

Next, start walking your right thumb over the trigger areas for the oesophagus and the stomach (see the adjoining diagram) in small steps, taking care not to omit even a smallest spot. During such probing, every time you encounter a sore spot, stop and give deep, alternating pressure for about a minute. In this manner, cover the entire trigger areas for the stomach and the oesophagus on the two feet.

Repeat this treatment twice a day.

(C) Pinching the web (skin) between the big and the second toes for a minute or two also helps.

(D) In very bad cases tie small rubber-bands on the big and the second toes of both the feet for 10-12 minutes. During this period, if a toe starts paining or turns black, remove the concerned band for a while (till the normal colour returns) and then reapply it. Repeat as often as required.

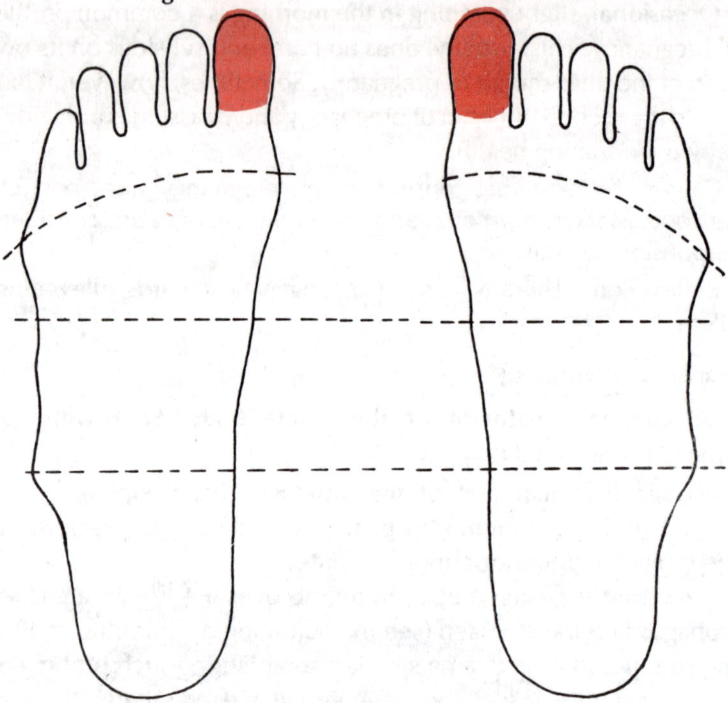

Fig. 11.5

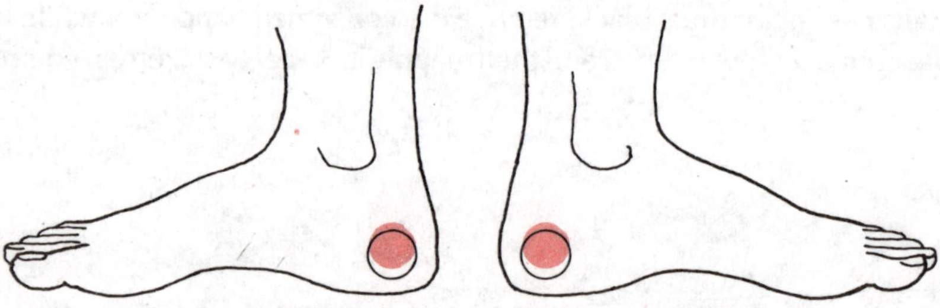

Fig. 11.6

FOR EASY DELIVERY

The logical conclusion of pregnancy is safe delivery of a healthy baby.

Delivery becomes imminent with the onset of labour pains. These are rhythmic, contractile pains which initially appear every 10 minutes. Each attack of pain lasts for about half a minute. Gradually, the interval between two pains shortens and the duration of each attack of pain lengthens. Finally, after 6 to 12 hours, a baby is born.

Reflex Zone Therapy is known to cut down the total period of labour almost by 50 per cent. With this treatment, there is a considerable decrease in pains but no dampening of uterine contractions or no inhibition of cervical dilatation. Moreover, Reflex Zone Therapy is known to hasten explusion of placenta, umbelical cord and after-births, after the baby is born. And the final point in favour of this therapy is that there is a complete absence of 'after-delivery exhaustion'.

Reflex Zone Therapy :

(A) **During the entire period of pregnancy,** the lady should roll her feet on a Reflex roller for 2-3 minutes, twice a day. This 'general' treatment helps to maintain good health.

(B) **When the labour pains start,** the trigger points for the mind and the uterus should be stimulated for about a minute each, with deep, alternating pressure.

Moreover, the lady should be given a comb to hold in each hand. During each attack of pain, she should press the thumb and the finger-tips against the teeth of the comb.

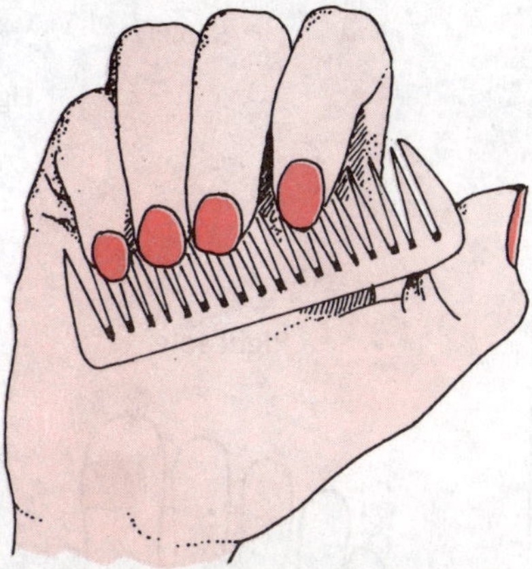

Fig. 11.7
Pressing teeth of comb into finger-tips.

(C) As the labour period draws to an end, tie small rubber-bands on the big and the second toes of both the feet and remove them after a couple of minutes. Continue this process till the baby has been born and 'after-births' have been expelled.

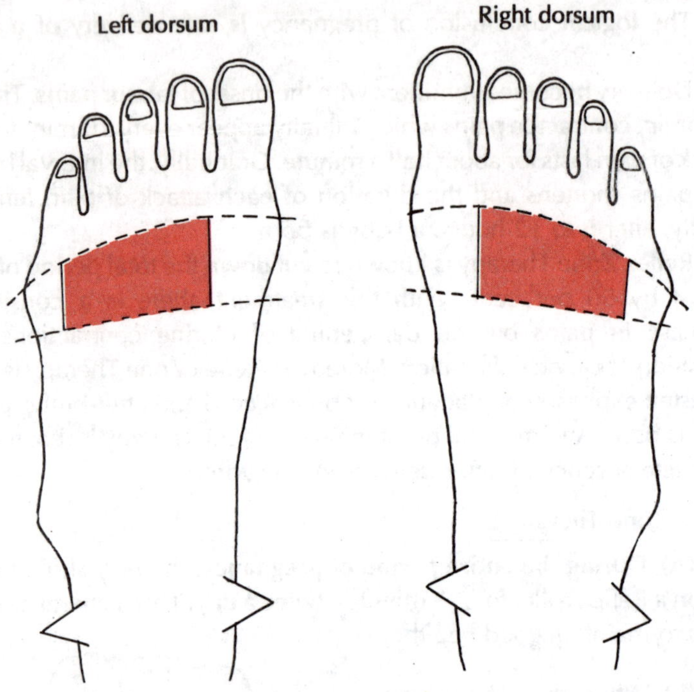

Fig. 11.8

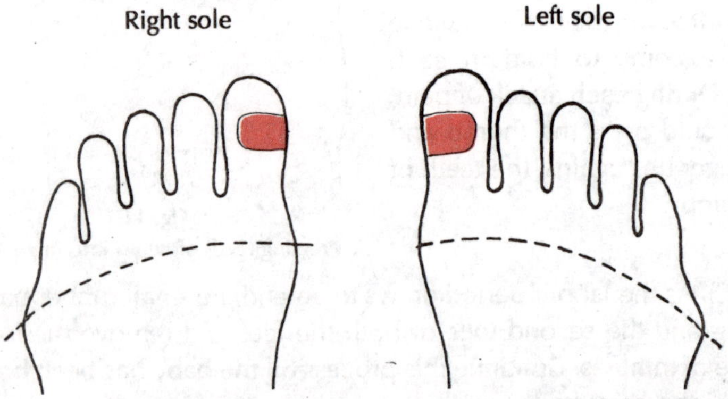

Fig. 11.9

PROBLEMS OF THE BREASTS

Pain; Lump/s; Deficiency of milk (Agalactia)

Breasts are present in males as well as females. However, in males they are present in a rudimentary form.

In females, they form an important part of the reproductive symptom. They develop after puberty and further increase in size during pregnancy and lactation.

Some women experience **pain and/or lumps in the breast/s,** especially before or during the menses.

During pregnancy, the breasts produce a yellowish fluid called colostrum. 2-3 days after the birth of the baby, a hormone prolactin, secreted by the pituitary gland, stimulates the breasts to produce milk.

Breast-milk is the best food for a baby because (1) it is sterile, (2) it is low in fats and high in sugar and (3) it imparts great immunity to the new-born. Breast-feeding is not only economical but also helps to develop a healthy mother-child relationship and acts as a natural contraceptive.

Unfortunately, many city-mothers suffer from a **deficiency of breast-milk,** exposing their children to risks of infection and obesity.

Reflex Zone Therapy :

(A) General treatment of the whole body : Start with general treatment as described on page 33.

(B) Specific treatment of the breasts : The breasts are represented on the dorsal (upper) surfaces of the two feet as shown in the adjoining diagram.

'Walk' your thumb over the trigger areas for the breasts in small steps, taking care not to omit even a smallest spot. During such probing, every time you encounter a sore spot, stop moving the thumb further and with its tip give deep, alternating pressure for about a minute. In this manner, cover the entire breast areas on the two feet.

Repeat this treatment twice a day.

(C) In agalactia also, stimulate the pituitary gland.

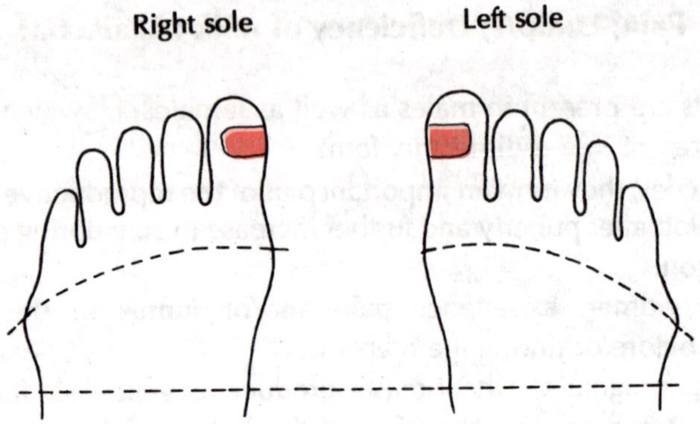

Fig. 11.10

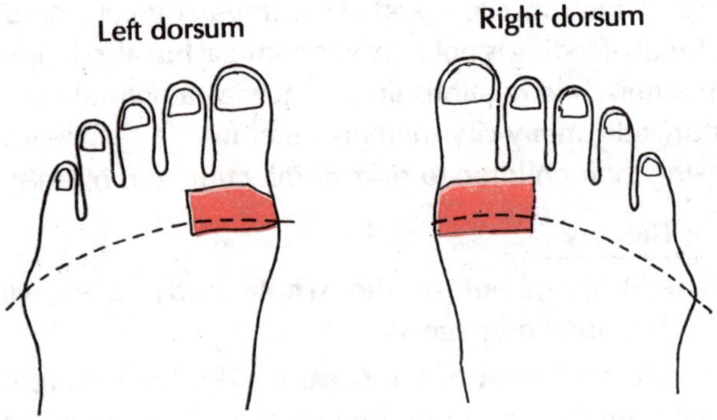

Fig. 11.11

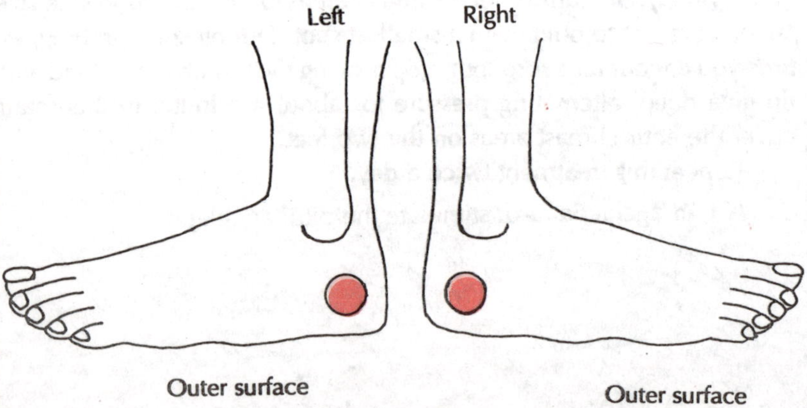

Fig. 11.12

MENOPAUSE

Menopause literally means cessation of menses. This marks the end of the reproductive life of a woman. This normal phenomenon usually occurs in late forties or early fifties but may occur much earlier or later.

For most women, this transition, from productive to non-productive life, is smooth and uneventful. However, a few women suffer from symptoms like–

1. Hot flushes, causing warmth in the face and ears
2. Sweating
3. Undue fatigue
4. Headaches
5. Dryness of the vagina
6. Easy irritability, inexplicable mood-changes and depression.

Usually, the above-mentioned symptoms subside on their own in a few months. Therefore, the only things such women require are rest and reassurance.

Women suffering from distressing symptoms are sometimes given sex hormones (hormone replacement therapy). However, a long-term use of such hormones is frought with danger of developing breast or cervical cancer. It is, therefore, wiser to rely on Reflex Zone Therapy to stimulate the glands producing sex hormones.

Reflex Zone Therapy :

(A) General treatment of the whole body : Start with general treatment as described on page 33.

(B) Specific treatment of the ovaries, the pituitary and the thyroid glands through deep and alternating pressure on trigger areas for each of these organs for about a minute, twice a day.

12. REFLEXOLOGY IN DISORDERS OF THE ENDOCRINE SYSTEM

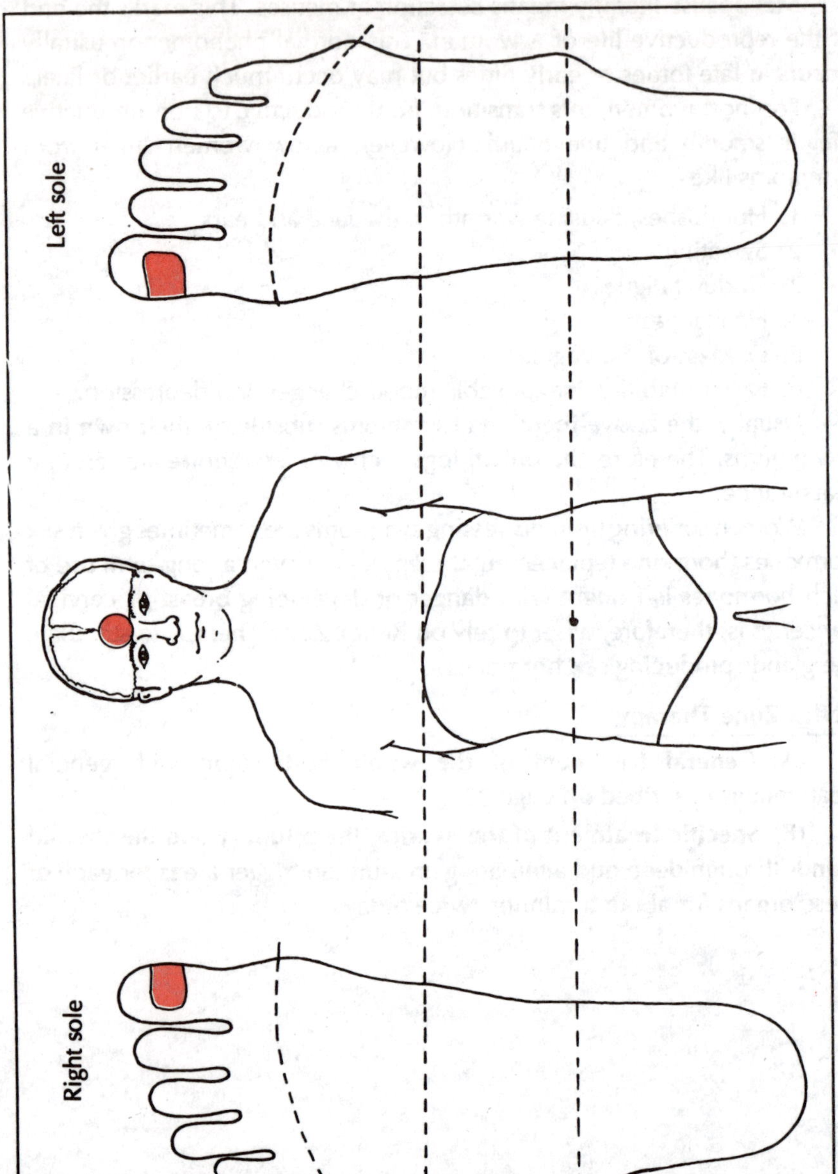

Fig. 12.1

PROBLEMS OF THE PITUITARY GLAND

Our body has two types of glands : **endocrine** and **exocrine.** Endocrine glands produce **hormones** and pour them directly into the blood. Exocrine glands produce **enzymes** that either remain confined within the producer cells or are poured into a body-cavity like the mouth, the stomach, etc.

Endocrine glands include 1 pituitary, 1 pineal, 1 thyroid, 4 parathyroids, 2 adrenals, 1 thymus, 1 pancreas, 2 ovaries in females or 2 testes in males.

The system of endocrine glands is controlled by (1) the hypothalamus (a part of the brain) and (2) the pituitary.

The pituitary is called the master gland of the body because it governs the activity of all other endocrine glands. It is a pea-shaped, reddish-brown gland that is situated just below the brain and is connected to the hypothalamus by a stalk.

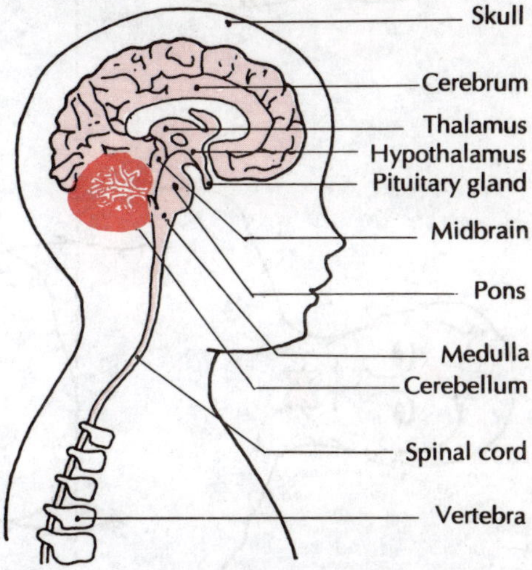

Fig. 12.2

The pituitary gland secretes a number of hormones viz. ACTH (controlling the adrenals), TSH (controlling the thyroid), LH + FSH (controlling the ovaries and the testes) and growth hormone (controlling the growth of the human body). A deficiency of growth hormone results in retarded physical growth **(dwarfism).**

A regular, mild stimulation of trigger spots for the pituitary (and other endocrine glands too) can go a long way towards the maintenance of health and youthfulness.

Reflex Zone Therapy :

(A) General treatment of the whole body : Start with general treatment as described on page 33.

(B) Specific treatment of the pituitary gland : Give deep and alternating pressure on the trigger spots for the pituitary on the two big toes (see the adjoining diagram) for about two minutes, twice a day.

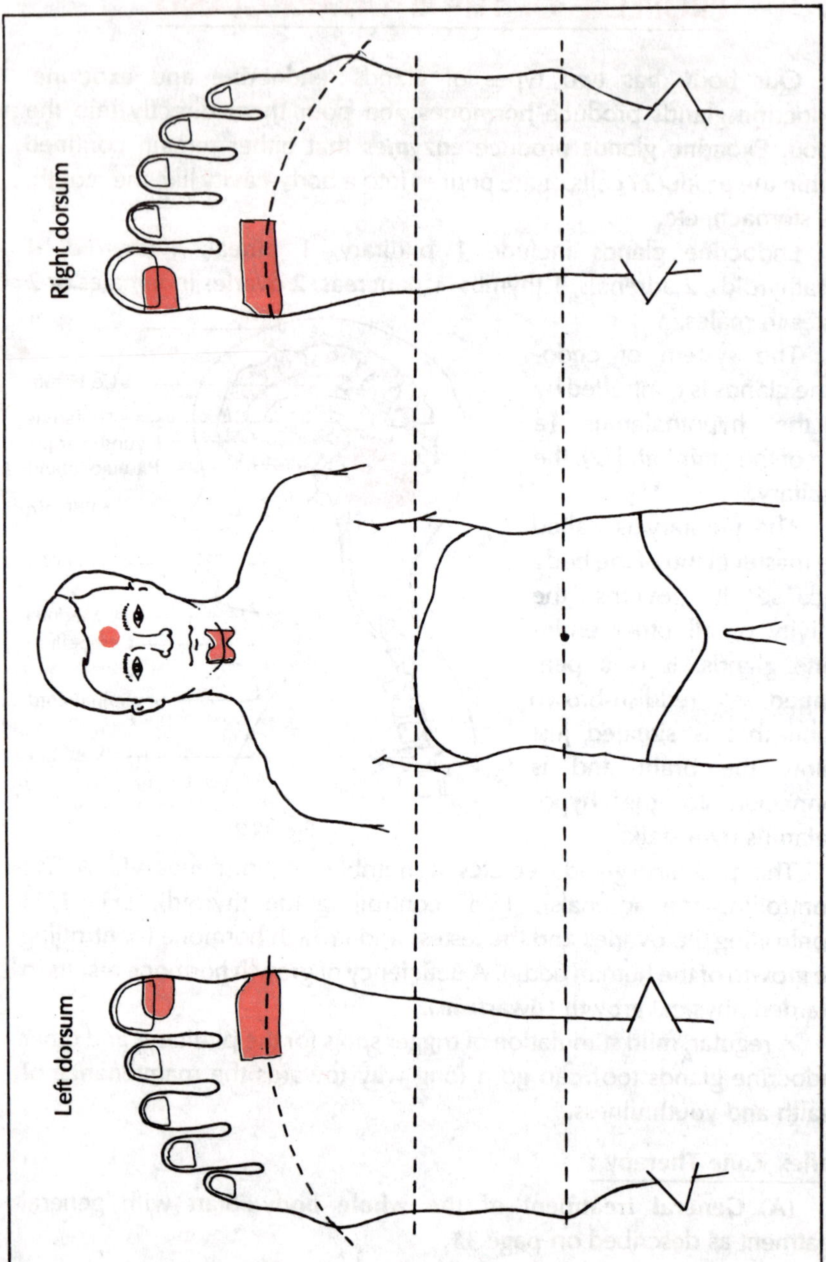

Fig. 12.2

DISORDERS OF THE THYROID GLAND

The thyroid is a 'H' or butterfly shaped endocrine gland, situated at the base of the front of the neck, overlying the voice box.

The hormones of the thyroid –

(1) are necessary for normal mental and physical development,

(2) are responsible for the body's metabolism, thereby controlling the 'basal metabolic rate'.

(3) are essential for the health of hair and skin.

Disorders of the thyroid include (a) underactivity or **hypothyroidism** and (b) overactivity or **hyperthyroidism.**

Their symptoms are tabulated below :

	Hypothyroidism	Hyperthyroidism
1	Incidence equal in both sexes	More common in females
2	Metabolic rate is slow	Metabolic rate is fast
3	Body is cool	Body is hot, due to which there is excess sweating
4	Tendency to gain weight in spite of meagre diet	Tendency to lose weight in spite of increased appetite
5	Blood pressure is low and pulse is slow	Blood pressure is high and pulse is rapid (always above 100/min)
6	Physical and mental lethargy (slowness)	Physical overactivity with trembling (esp. of the fingers) and nervous tension

Reflex Zone Therapy :

(A) General treatment of the whole body : Start with general treatment as described on page 33.

(B) Specific treatment of the thyroid and the pituitary glands : Grasp (pinch) the thyroid area on any one big toe with the thumb and the index finger and give deep, alternating pressure for about a minute.

Similarly, stimulate the trigger area for the thyroid on the other big toe.

Next, deeply press the trigger areas for the pituitary gland (at the centres of big toes) for about a minute each.

Repeat this treatment twice a day.

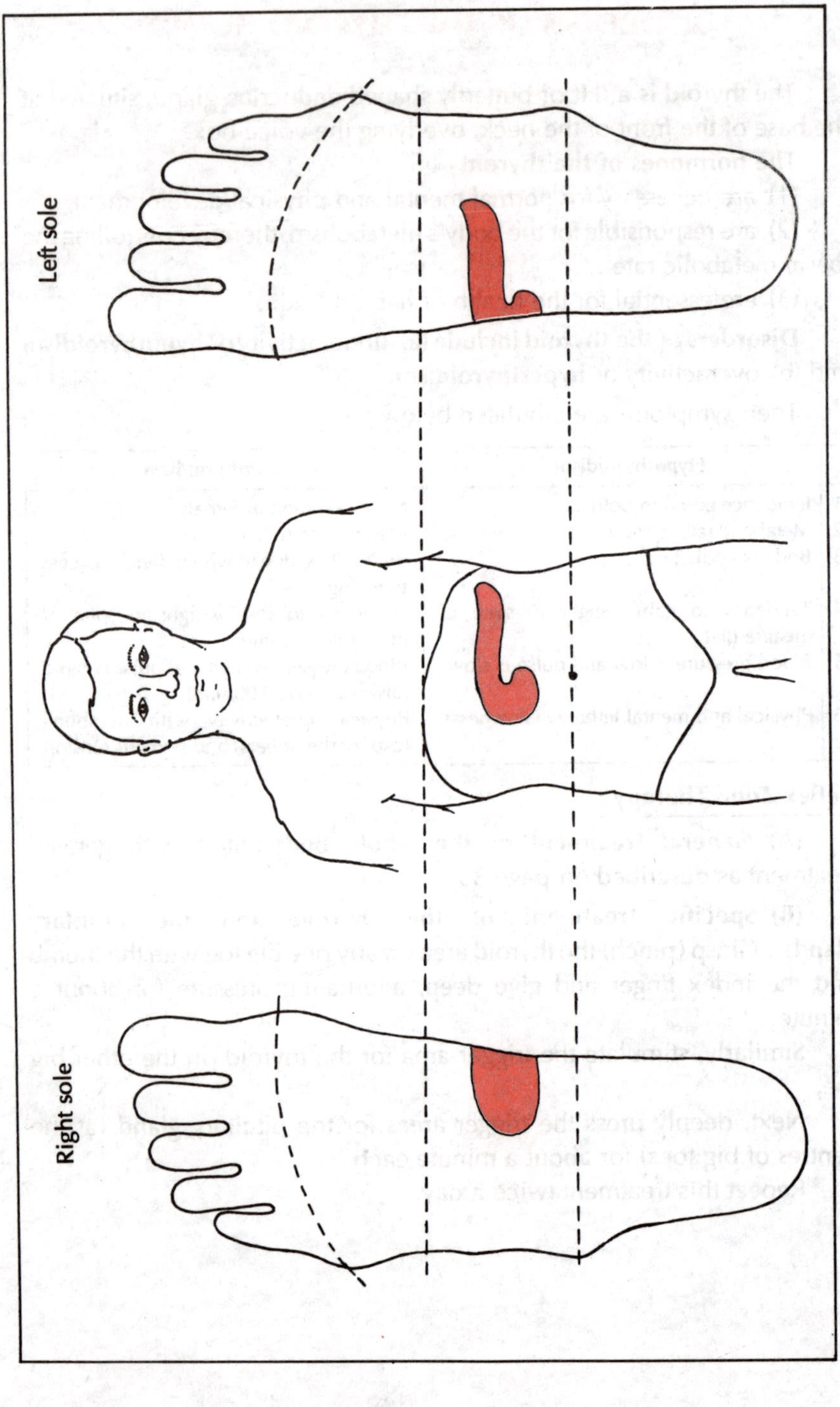

Fig. 12.3

PROBLEMS OF THE PANCREAS

Diabetes mellitus

Diabetes is an endocrine disorder resulting from either (a) relative or absolute deficiency or (b) resistance of body-cells to insulin, the hormone secreted by the pancreas.

Each cell of our body requires glucose for its survival. Insulin pumps glucose present in the blood into the cells of the body. In absence of insulin, glucose cannot enter the cells and, therefore, accumulates in the blood (hyperglycemia). When the concentration of glucose in the blood exceeds a particular limit, it overflows into the urine. This justifies the Sanskrit name of Diabetes : **Madhumeha** (a shower of honey).

Uncontrolled diabetes produces three classical symptoms : excessive hunger, excessive thirst and excessive urine. Other common symptoms include : recurrent boils, failure of wounds to heal, frequent changes in spectacle-glass numbers and itching about the genitals.

Diabetes is an incurable disease. It can only be controlled. Therefore, treatment has to be continued throughout life. Here Reflex Zone Therapy assumes a special importance.

Reflex Zone Therapy :

(A) General treatment of the whole body : Start with general treatment as described on page 33.

(B) Specific treatment of the pancreas : Carefully observe the 'pancreas areas' on the two feet and then visualize them on your own feet. If necessary, delineate them with a pen.

Place the left foot on the right thigh. Start 'walking' the right thumb on the pancreas area in small steps, taking care not to omit even a smallest spot. During such probing, every time you encounter a sore spot, stop moving the thumb further and with its tip, give deep alternating pressure for about a minute.

After covering the entire pancreas area on the left foot, reverse the positions of the legs and in a similar manner, stimulate the trigger areas for the pancreas on the right foot.

Repeat this treatment twice a day, preferably about an hour after each meal.

13. REFLEXOLOGY IN DISORDERS OF THE SENSE ORGANS

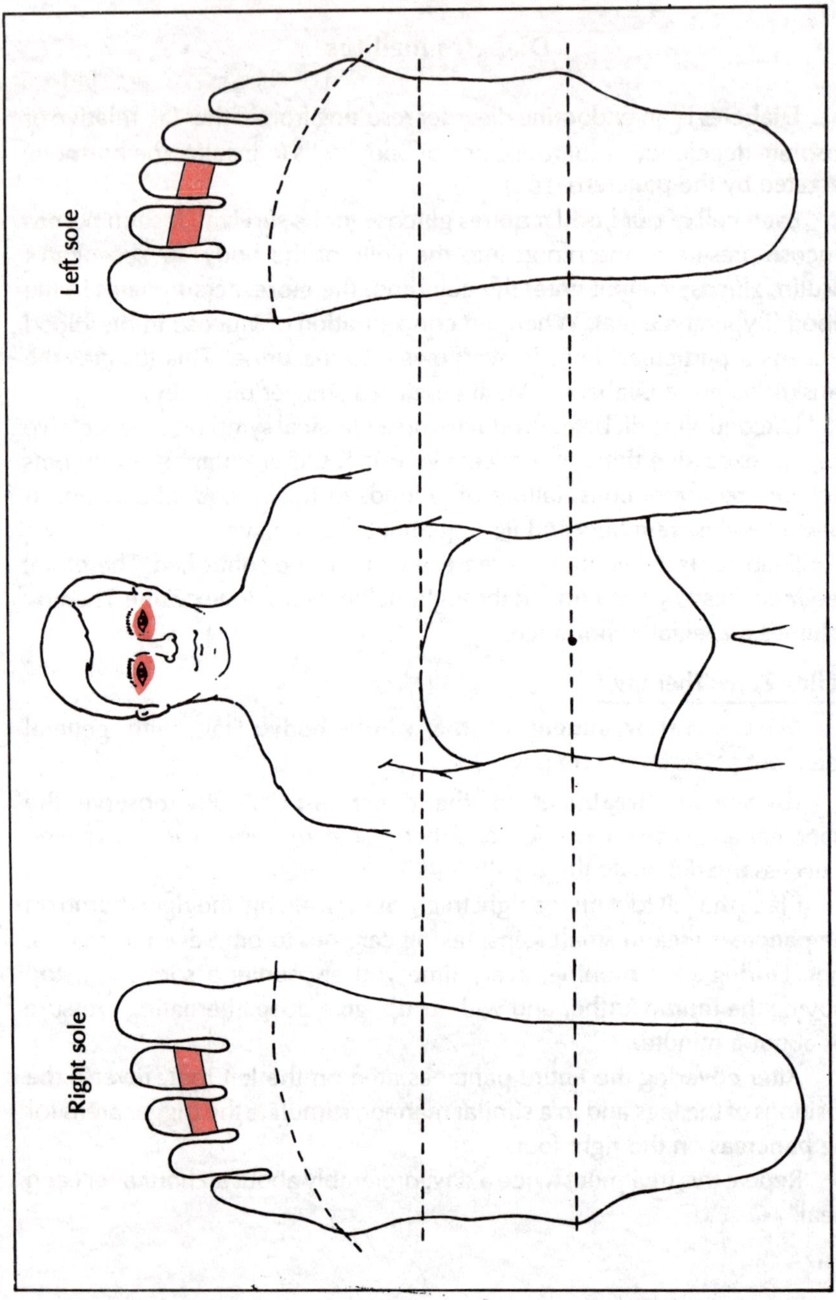

Fig. 13.1

PROBLEMS OF THE EYES

The eyes are, perhaps, the most important of all sense organs. Indeed, more than 80% of information we possess about the world is gathered through the eyes.

Unfortunately, the eyes are the most abused of all organs. They are at ease when we look at distance. But we seldom allow them to do so, engaging them in close-range activities like reading and writing hour after hour. It is no wonder that eye and visual defects like **squint, short sightedness** and **astigmatism** are all on the rise.

Eyes are also liable to contract infections. The eyes, then, become red and may pain. Eye-infections can be classified into superficial (e.g., **conjunctivitis**) and deep (e.g., **iritis, cyclitis, retinitis** etc.). The two varieties can be differentiated from each other by the nature of redness. Moreover, in conjunctivitis, there is a discharge of pus from the eyes, which glues the lids to each other.

Another common eye-disease, usually affecting the elderly, is **cataract.** Here, the lens present in the eye loses its transparency and gradually grows opaque, causing progressive diminishing of vision.

Reflex Zone Therapy :

(A) General treatment of the whole body : Start with general treatment as described on page 33.

(B) Specific treatment of the eyes : The eyes are represented on the second and the third toes as shown in the adjoining diagram.

Using the thumb and the first finger, press upon the upper and lower surfaces of the concerned areas of the first and the second toe and then the third toe for about a minute each. Give deep, alternating pressure. Similarly, stimulate the trigger areas for the eyes on the other foot.

Repeat this treatment twice a day.

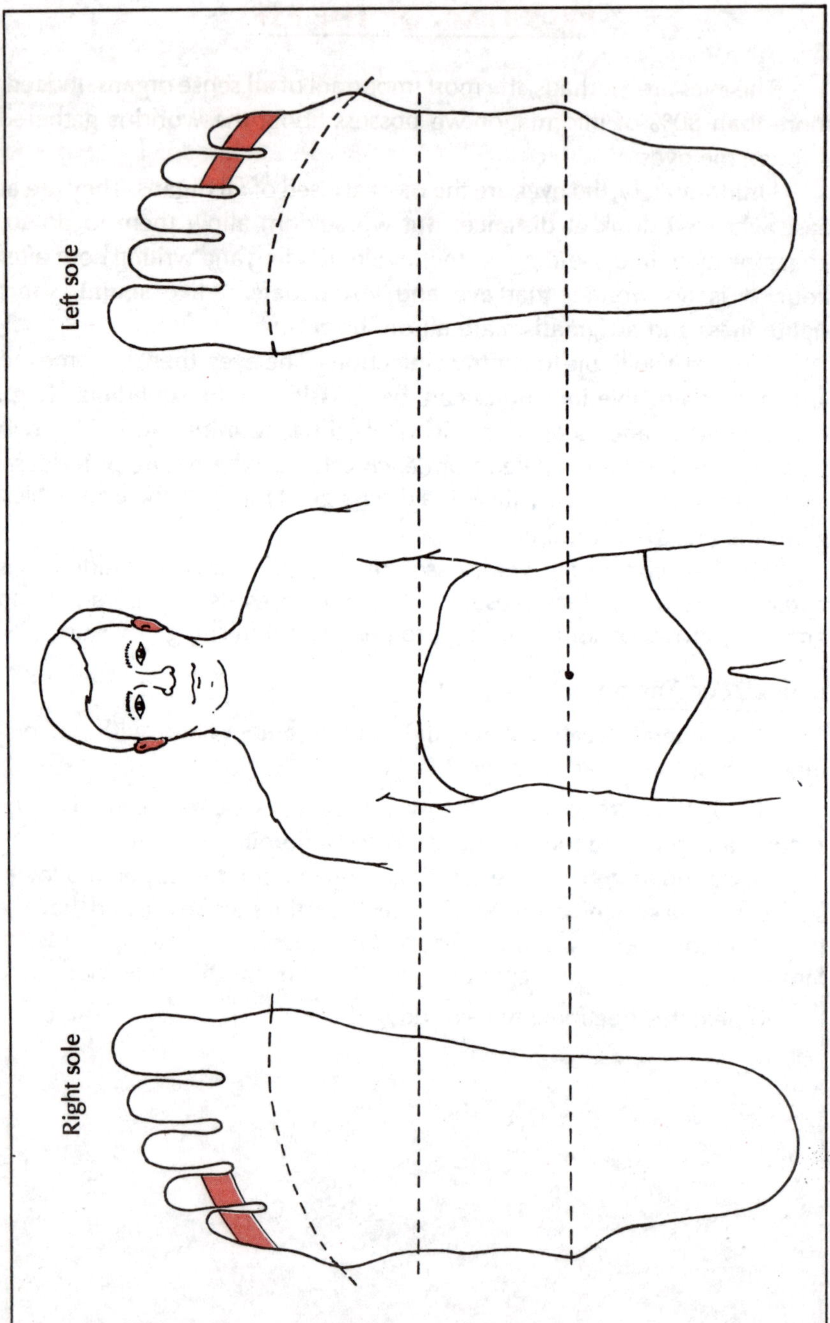

Fig. 13.2

PROBLEMS OF THE EAR

We all know that ears are organs of hearing. But, not many know that ears are also concerned with the balancing of the body.

There is more to an ear than meets the eye. Only a small part of the ear is externally visible. This part, called pinna, is a part of the 'external ear'. The parts of the ear, not externally visible are the 'middle ear' and the 'internal ear'.

The middle ear is, frequently, a victim of infection and inflammation (swelling). This is called **'otitis media'.** Occasionally, external or internal ear may get inflammed (**otitis externa** and **otitis interna,** respectively).

In ear problems, one or more of the following symptoms may be present :

1. Pain in the ear, which could be very severe.
2. Discharge of watery, bloody or pus-like fluid from the ear.
3. Loss of hearing.
4. Noises (ringing or whistling) in the ear.
5. Vertigo, a sensation of the world swirling around.

Reflex Zone Therapy :

(A) General treatment of the whole body : Start with general treatment as described on page 33.

(B) Specific treatment of the ear : The right ear is represented on the right foot whereas the left ear is represented on the left foot (see the adjoining diagram).

Give deep, alternating pressure, both on the upper and lower surfaces (by using the thumb and the index finger) of the 4th and the 5th toes for about a minute each.

Repeat this treatment twice a day.

(C) For very severe pain in the ear, tie small rubber-bands on the 4th and the 5th toes of the same side for 10-12 minutes. During this period, if a toe starts aching or turns blue, remove the concerned rubber-band for a while (till the normal colour returns), and then reapply it.

Repeat every hour till the pain subsides.

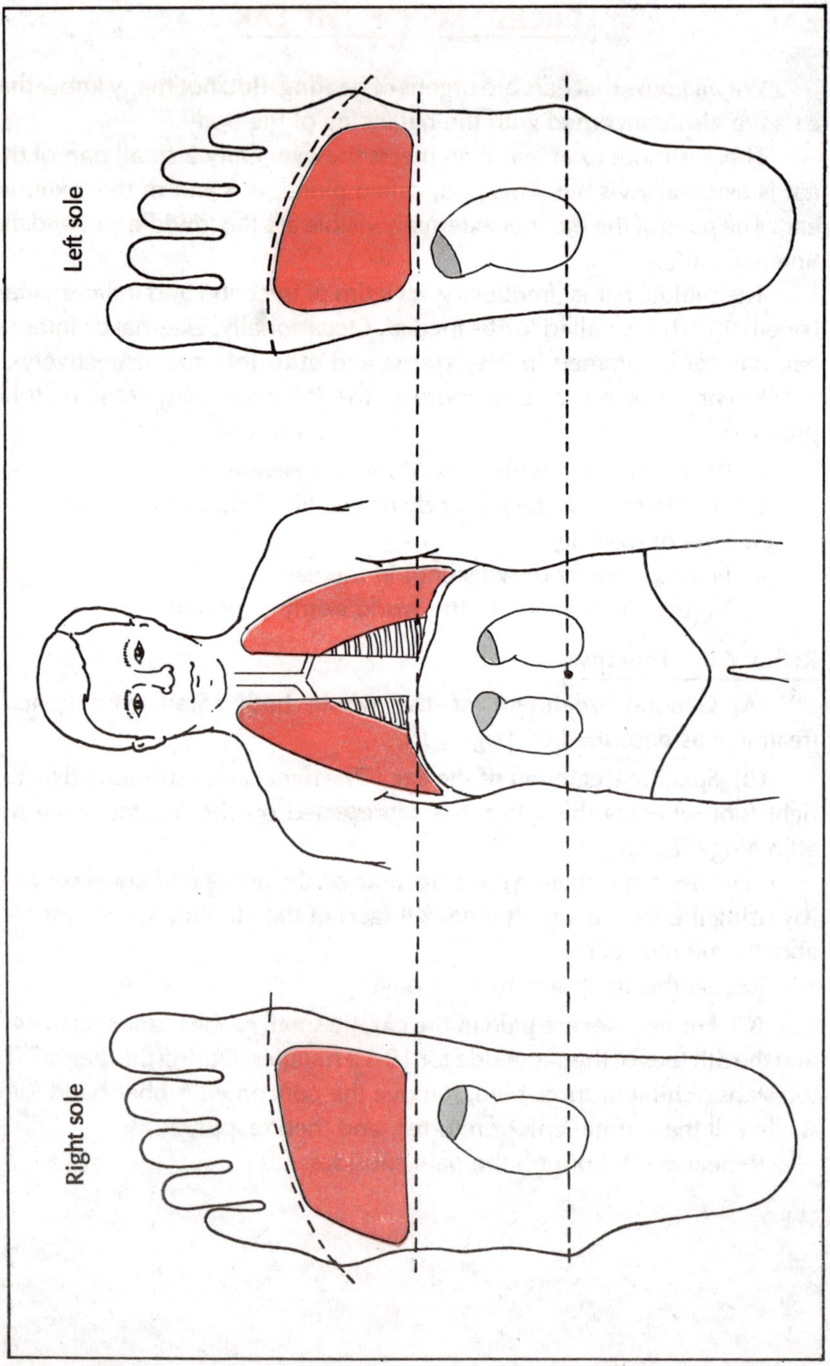

Fig. 13.3

PROBLEMS OF THE SKIN

The skin is a strong, elastic membrane that encloses the body and protects it from damage by injury or infection. An average man is covered by approximately 18 square feet of skin, which weighs about 4 kg. It varies in thickness from 0.05 to 5 mm. The thickest skin is found on the palms and soles whereas the thinnest is found on the eye-lids. The skin contains innumerable sweat glands, again varying in number from part to part of the body. On palms or soles, there are about 3000 sweat glands per square inch. On the back, they are sparse, numbering about 500 per square inch. Sensations of pain, touch and temperature are conveyed to the brain by nerve-endings in the skin. Skin also has oil-producing sebaceous glands. This oil protects the skin and keeps it supple. Deficiency of this oil (sebum) causes cracking of the skin, esp. in winter.

Apart from covering and thereby protecting the body and its organs, skin serves three other important functions : (1) it aids in regulating body-temperature, (2) it helps to excrete waste products through sweat and (3) it manufactures vitamin D when exposed to sunlight.

Common skin-problems include–

Scabies, which is an infectious disease characterized by intense itching, especially between finger and on groins.

Eczema, which is an allergic disease characterized by redness, itching, oozing and finally thickening of the skin.

Even in other skin-problems, the treatment specified below will help.

Reflex Zone Therapy :

(A) General treatment of the whole body : Start with general treatment as described on page 33.

(B) Specific treatment of the affected area of the body through deep, alternating pressure on the corresponding part/s of the feet, twice a day.

(C) Specific treatment of the lungs and the adrenal glands since these are related with the health of the skin.

14. REFLEXOLOGY IN SOME OTHER COMMON DISORDERS

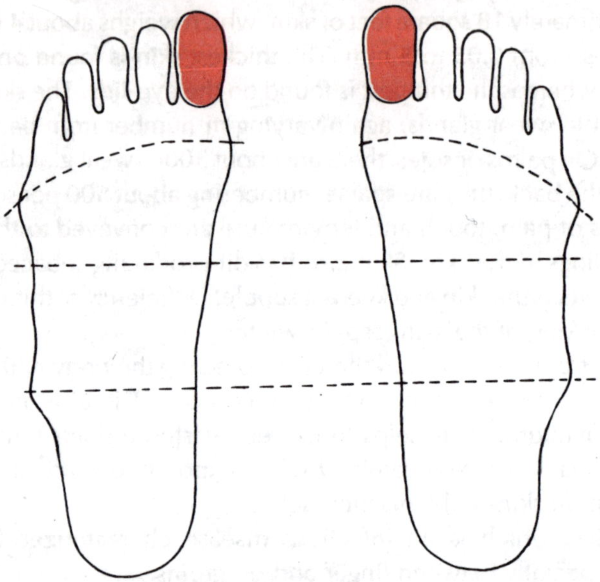

Fig. 14.1

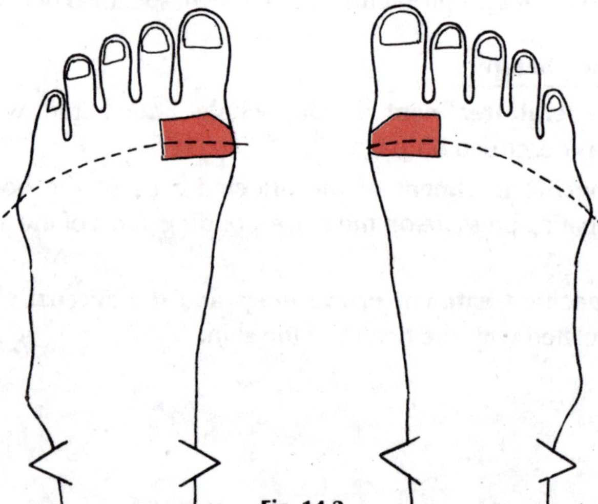

Fig. 14.2

OBESITY

Bernard Shaw has said that there is no love more sincere than the love of food. Indeed, out of a sheer love for food, man overeats and grows fat.

The word 'obesity' has been derived from the Latin word 'obesus' which means to eat away, to devour. Obviously, it is the result of overeating or more precisely of an imbalance between the input and output of energy.

There are numerous hazards of obesity. Fat persons are more likely to suffer from diabetes, high blood pressure, ischemic heart disease and a host of other diseases. Studies have shown that every 10 per cent extra weight clips 13 per cent off one's life.

All causes of obesity are not yet clear. Genetic factors and hormonal imbalances have been blamed. However, even these factors can't operate unless energy (food) input is in excess of energy output (through physical exercise).

Reflex Zone Therapy :

(A) General treatment of the whole body : Start with general treatment as described on page 33.

(B) Specific treatment of the brain/mind and the thyroid through deep and alternating pressure on the trigger areas for these organs for about a minute each, twice a day. When stimulating the thyroid area, use the thumb (on the upper surface of the big toe) and the first finger (on the lower surface of the big toe) to give pinching pressure.

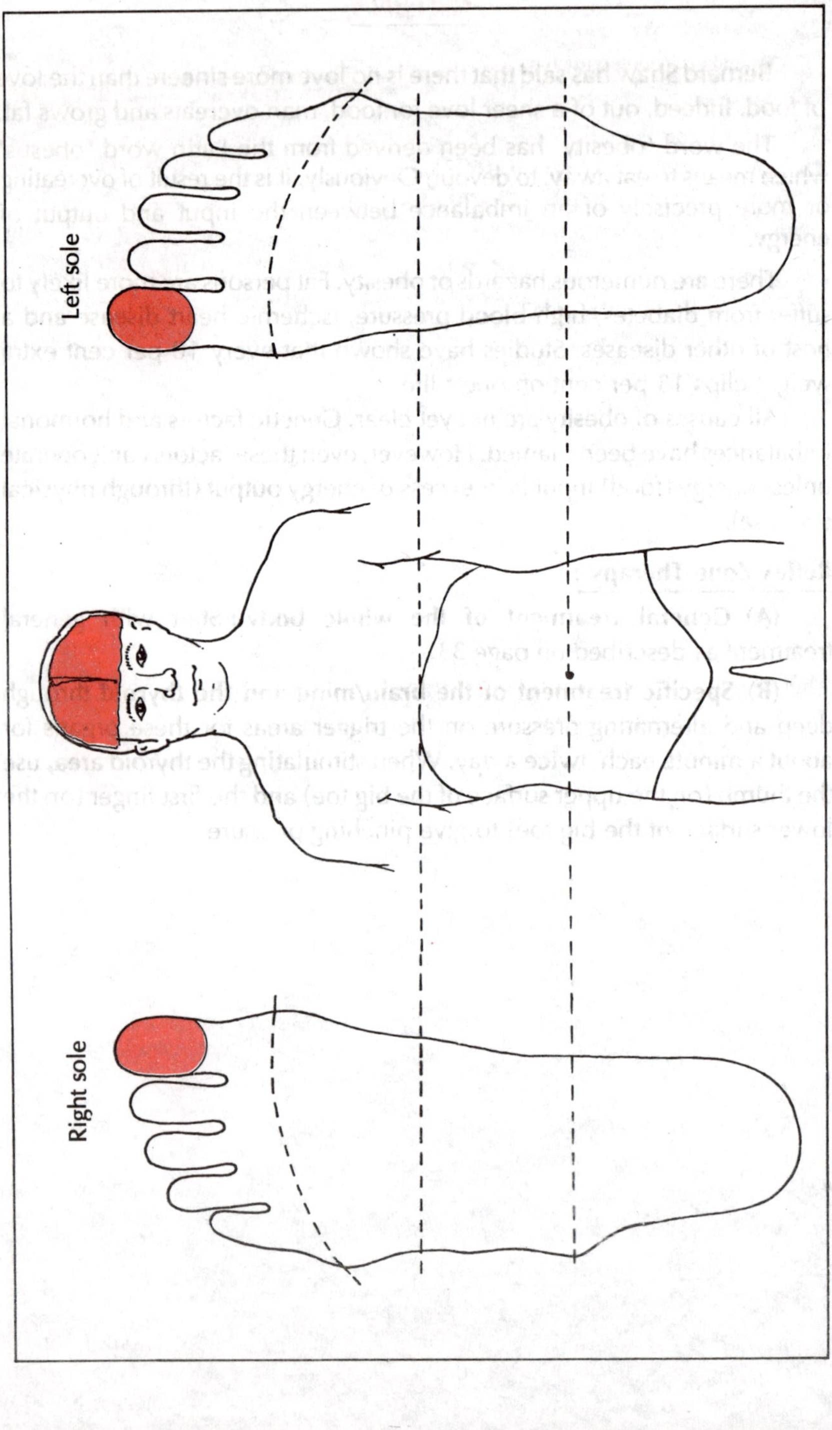

Fig. 14.3

FEVER

Fever is a word that frightens most people. They run helter-skelter for medical help at the first signs of fever, thinking it to be a great enemy. We fail to understand the origin of such an erroneous concept about fever.

The fact is : **Fever is a friend, not a foe.** It is body's defence against disease. Whenever a part of the body is invaded by disease-causing micro-organisms like bacteria or viruses, the body produces chemicals called pyrogens which raise the body's temperature. This activates the white cells present in the blood which rush to the affected part to destroy the concerned micro-organisms. In other words, a rising body-temperature simply indicates that the process of healing has begun in right earnest. It is something to rejoice over, not panic. Artificially induced fevers have been used in laboratory experiments on animals to demonstrate this process. Elevated temperatures decrease the death-rate among animals infected with disease, but if their body-temperatures are lowered, most of them die.

Therefore, when you (or one of your kins) next suffer from fever, don't rush for 'over-the-counter' medicines like aspirin or paracetamol. Such measures are actually self-defeating. Fever should be allowed to run its own course. Rest assured that fever cannot rise inexorably. There are regulating centres in the brain which prevent body-temperature from going above 105° F.

Albeit, we do not mean to say that you should not take or seek treatment when affected with fever. But, the treatment should be directed at the disease which is causing fever. Usually, fever accompanies obvious diseases like colds, sinusitis, tonsillitis, sore throat, lung diseases, etc.

Reflex Zone Therapy :

(A) General treatment of the whole body : Start with general treatment as described on page 33.

(B) Specific treatment of the brain and the hypothalamus : These organs are represented on the two big toes as shown in the adjoining diagram.

Start 'walking' your thumb on these trigger areas, in small steps, taking care not to omit even a smallest spot. During such probing, every time you encounter a sore spot, stop moving the thumb further and with its tip, give deep alternating pressure for about a minute.

Repeat this treatment every hour, till the body-temperature comes down considerably.

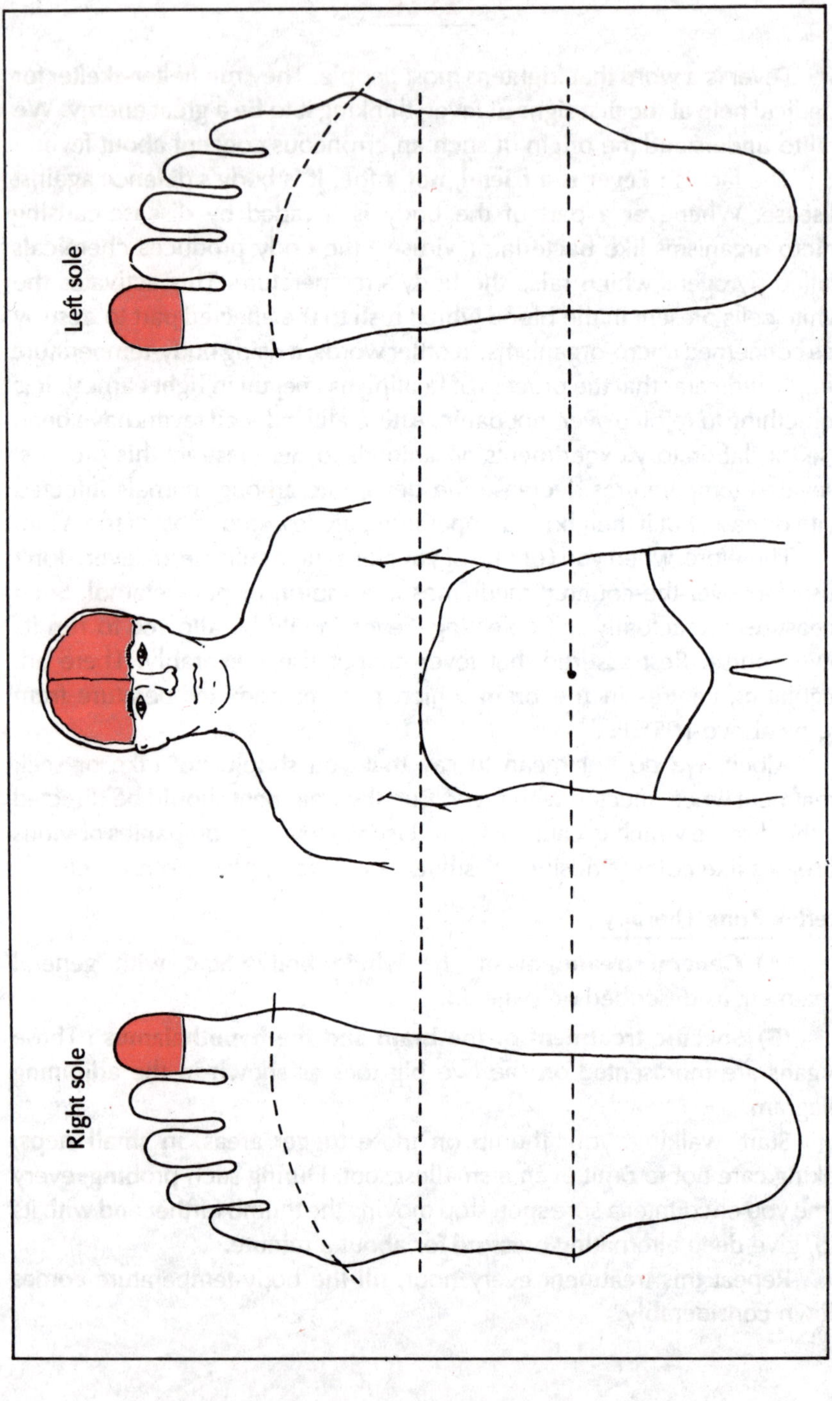

Fig. 14.4

PROBLEMS OF THE MIND

Mental tension; Sleeplessness; Forgetfulness

Stressful situations are inevitable in today's modern, competitive life. However, circumstances themselves can do us little harm. It is our incorrect response to circumstances that does harm. Indeed, a host of disorders have been attributed to **mental stress.** Headaches, insomnia, high blood pressure, hyperacidity, peptic ulcers are all on the rise.

Sleeplessness is a natural consequence of modernization. There are no rules to decide how much sleep is necessary for the well-being of a person. Most people sleep 7-8 hours each night, but 8% are satisfied with 5 hours or less and 4% want 10 hours or more. Normal sleep is made up of two distinct, alternating phases : orthodox sleep (occurring early in the night) and paradoxical (REM) sleep which is associated with dreaming. Both phases are essential for good health. Most sleeping tablets suppress the REM phase. Another serious drawback of sleeping pills is that they are habit-forming.

Common causes of sleeplessness include : (1) Worry and anxiety, (2) Noise, (3) Lack of bodily fatigue due to a sedentary life, (4) digestive upsets or bodily pain, (5) consumption of stimulants like tea or coffee and (6) an irregular life.

Causes of **forgetfulness** are difficult to pinpoint. We tend to forget things that don't interest us. Forgetfulness in old age is the result of a degeneration of brain cells.

Reflex Zone Therapy :

(A) General treatment of the whole body : Start with general treatment as described on page 33.

(B) Specific treatment of the mind/brain through deep, alternating pressure on the trigger areas for the mind/brain (see the adjoining diagram) on the big toes, for about two minutes each.

Repeat this treatment twice a day.

(C) Just before going to sleep, firmly clench the teeth and tightly clasp (interlock) the fingers for as long as possible. This releases physical tension.

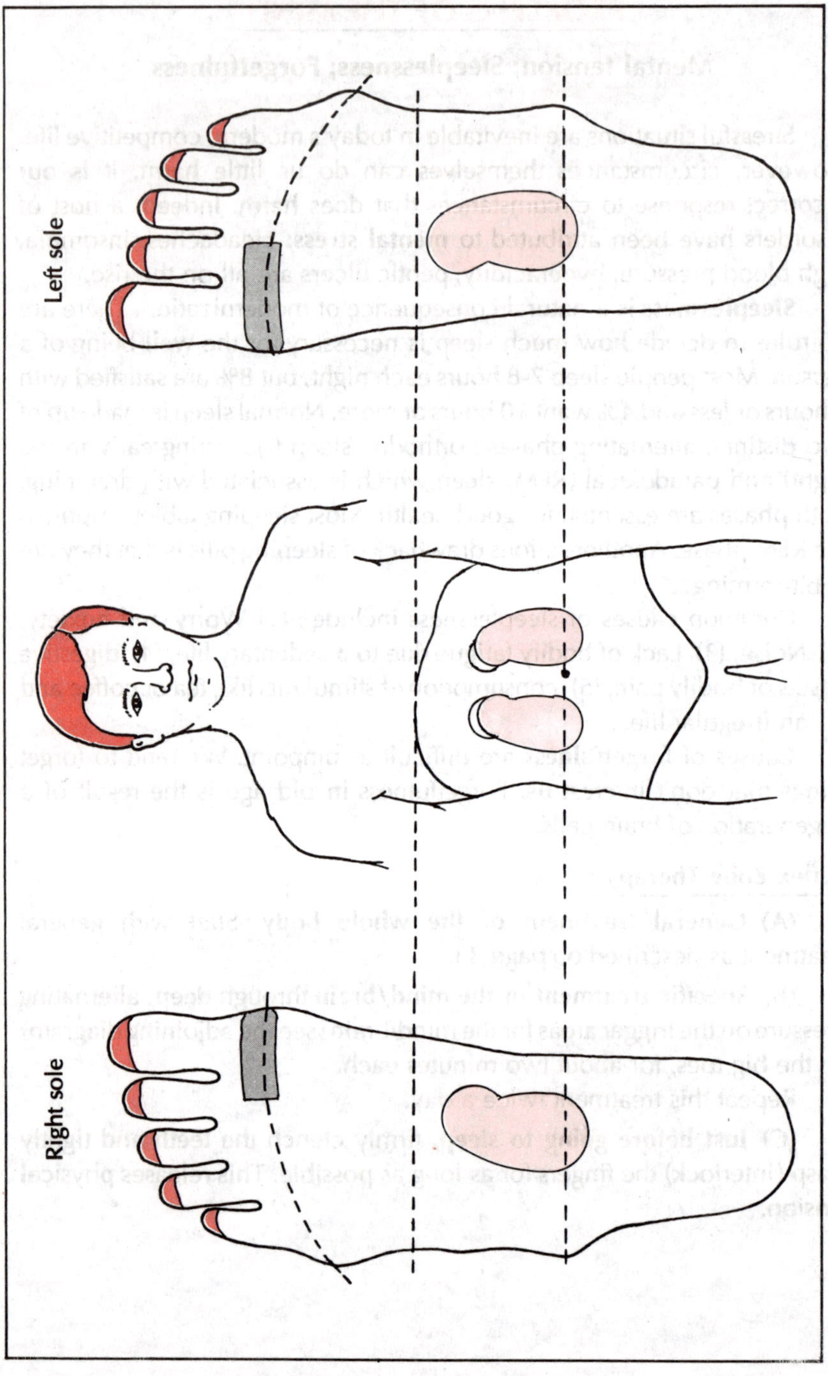

Fig. 14.5

PROBLEMS OF THE HAIR

Hair serves a protective function in animals. Not only does it keep away insects but also traps air to form an insulating envelope around the body.

The ancestors of human beings had considerable hair on their bodies. But as man resorted to the use of clothes, his hair grew small and sparse. Indeed, in human beings, hair is now considered vestigeal.

The black colour of our hair is because of a pigment called melanin. When this is replaced by tiny molecules of air, the hair appears grey or white.

Hair is considered by many, a mirror of the body. Indeed, factors that undermine general health also adversely affect the hair. Malnutrition, protein deficiency, anaemia, prolonged fevers, thyroid disorders, mental shock or stress all result into loss or greying of hair. However, a mild hair-fall every day is normal and should cause no concern.

Other disorders of hair include dandruff and lice.

Reflex Zone Therapy :

(A) General treatment of the whole body : Start with general treatment as described on page 33.

(B) Specific treatment of the head, the thyroid and the kidneys (see the adjoining diagram).

(i) Give deep, alternating pressure on the tip of each toe for about half a minute, twice a day. Alternatively you may press upon the fingers.

(ii) 'Walk' your thumb on the trigger areas for the thyroid and the kidneys in small steps, taking care not to omit even a smallest spot. During such probing, every time you encounter a sore spot, stop moving the thumb further and with its tip give deep, alternating pressure for about a minute.

Repeat this treatment twice a day.

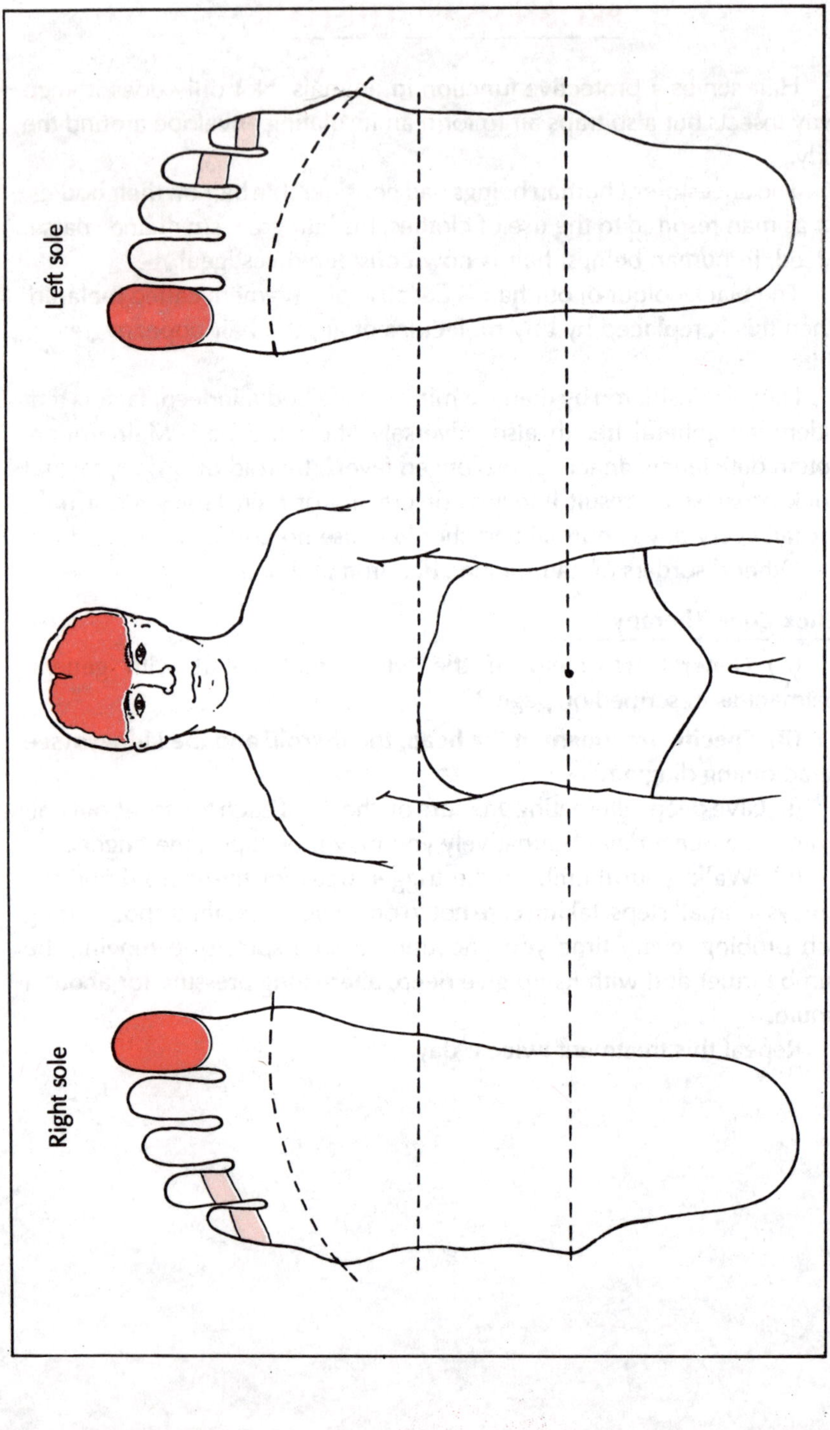

Fig. 14.6

GIDDINESS (VERTIGO)

Vertigo can be defined as a feeling of rotation or movement of one's self or of the surroundings.

Frequently, vertigo is caused by an ear problem. But sometimes it may be the result of head injury, a sudden rise of blood pressure or a disturbance of blood supply to the brain. Some people suffer it while travelling in a ship or a vehicle (travel sickness).

This extremely distressing symptom is many a time accompanied by nausea and vomiting, and is made worse by movement of the head.

Reflex Zone Therapy :

(A) General treatment of the whole body : Start with general treatment as described on page 33.

(B) Specific treatment of the brain and the ears through deep, alternating pressure on the trigger spots for these organs (see the adjoining organ) for about a minute each, whenever an attack of vertigo strikes. For a chronic problem, take treatment twice a day.

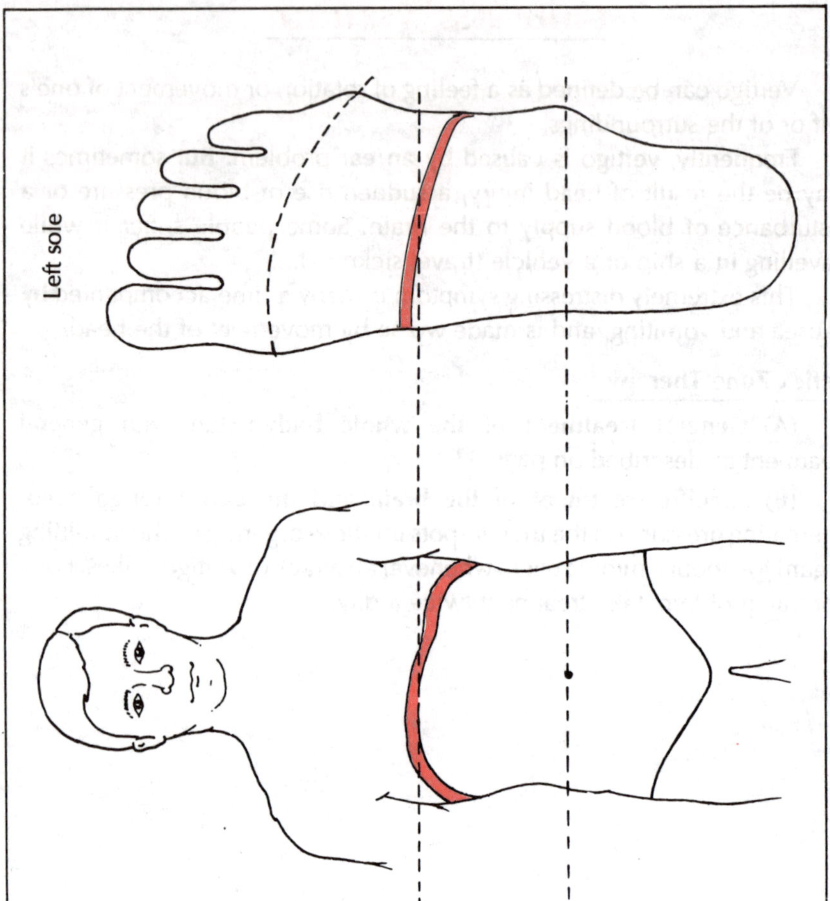

Fig. 14.7

HICCUPS

Diaphragm is a dome-shaped respiratory muscle present at the base of the chest. When it contracts, it moves down, the volume of the chest increases and, therefore, air is drawn into the lungs. When it relaxes, it moves up, pushing the air out. These processes occur in a gentle, peaceful manner.

Hiccups are involuntary, recurrent sounds produced when air forcefully passes through the vocal cords, following violent contractions of the diaphragm due to irritation. Such irritation is usually caused by consumption of excessively spicy food or alcohol and by choking.

According to an Indian superstition, one gets hiccups when a distant beloved is intensely thinking of him! How we wish this were true!

Hiccups, usually, subside on their own. Drinking water or holding the breath helps. If, however, they refuse to subside, Reflex Zone Therapy may help.

Reflex Zone Therapy :

(A) General treatment of the whole body : Start with general treatment as described on page 33.

(B) Specific treatment of the diaphragm : The diaphragm is represented in the form of a transverse band across the two feet.

Place the left foot on the right thigh. Start walking the right thumb along this trigger band for the diaphragm, in small steps, taking care not to omit even a smallest spot. During such probing, every time you encounter a sore spot, stop moving the thumb further and with its tip give deep, alternating pressure for about a minute.

After covering the entire trigger band for the diaphragm on the left foot, reverse the positions of the legs and in a similar manner, stimulate the trigger band for the diaphragm on the right foot.

(C) In resistant cases : Clasp (interlock) the fingers of the two hands tightly. Maintain firm pressure as long as hiccups continue. Alternatively, tie rubber-bands on all toes for about 10-12 minutes. During this period, if a toe starts aching or turns blue, remove the concerned rubber-band for a while (till the normal colour returns) and then reapply it.

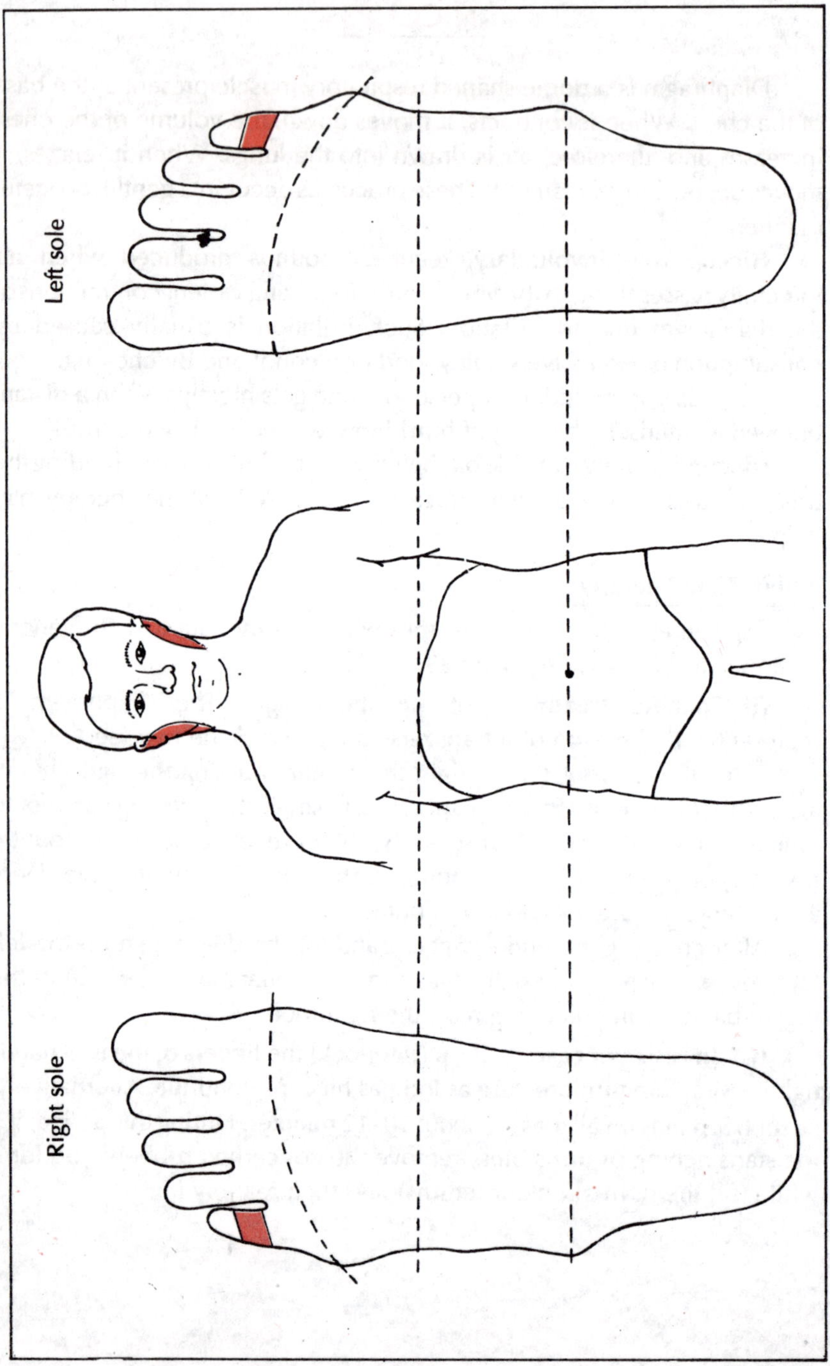

Fig. 14.8

MUMPS

Mumps is a disease of children and young adults, characterized by a hard swelling over one or both cheeks due to a viral infection of the parotid (salivary) glands. This is accompanied by fever and pain in the affected cheek/s.

Mumps occurring after puberty is a cause for concern because the viruses may travel to the testes, causing orchitis. A damage to both the testes may result into sterility.

Mumps being a viral disease, there is no cure with conventional medicines. Medicines are given only to alleviate distressing symptoms like fever, pain or swelling. Here, Reflex Zone Therapy may play a significant role in hastening recovery and preventing complications.

Reflex Zone Therapy :

(A) General treatment of the whole body : Start with general treatment as described on page 33.

(B) Specific treatment of the affected cheek : Observe the adjoining diagram to understand where the cheek is represented on the little toe.

Using the thumb and the first finger firmly press (in an alternating manner) the trigger area for the affected cheek, for about two minutes.

Repeat this treatment twice a day.

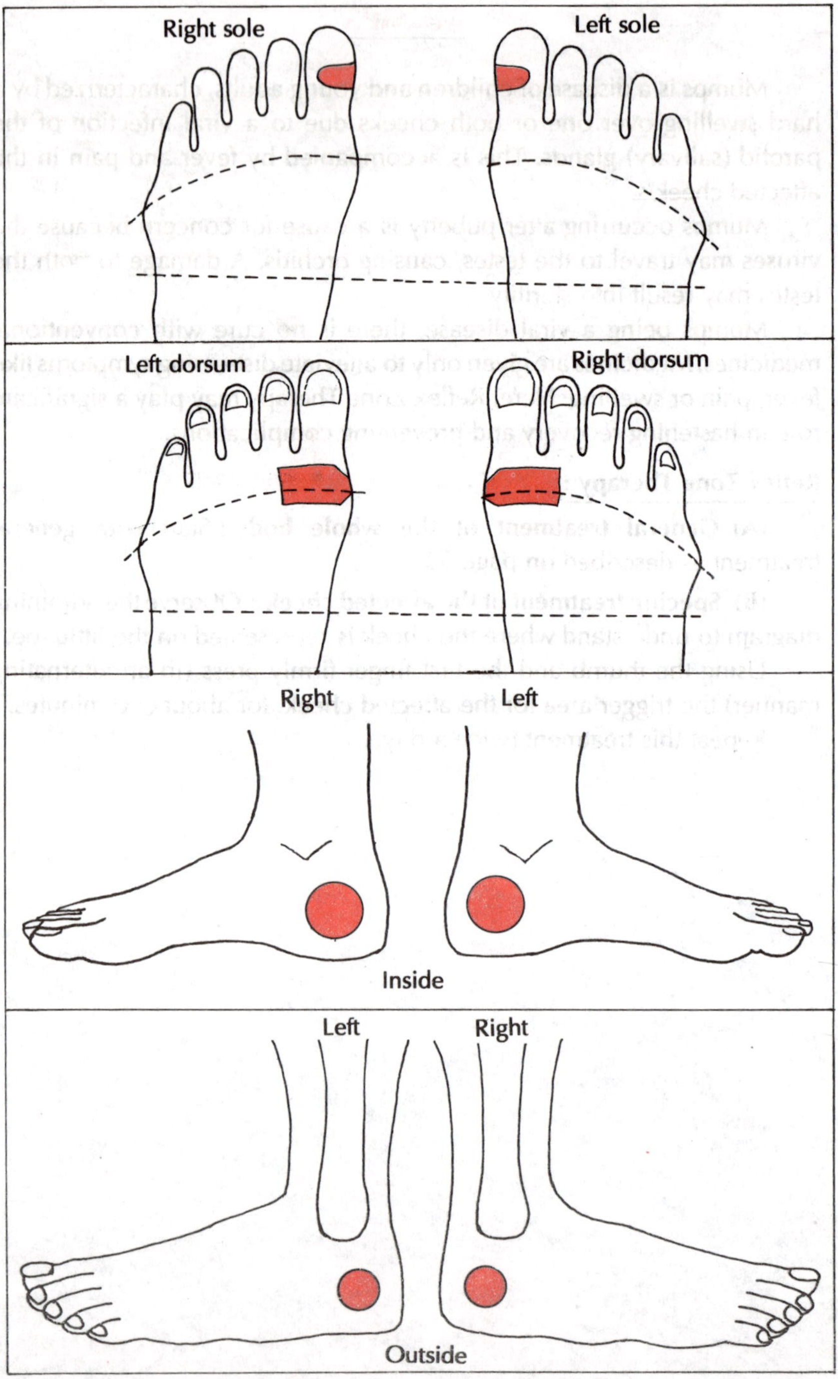
Right sole
Left sole
Left dorsum
Right dorsum
Right
Left
Inside
Left
Right
Outside

15. GENERAL DEBILITY/CHRONIC FATIGUE

Diseases like jaundice, typhoid, malaria, anaemia leave in their wake, a state of exhaustion and general weakness.

Other factors that contribute to general debility are : irregular life, incorrect dietary habits, lack of physical exercise and addictions.

Chronic mental tension, which is the natural consequence of today's hectic and competitive life is the chief cause of chronic fatigue.

Reflex Zone Therapy :

(A) General treatment of the whole body : Start with general treatment as detailed on page 33

(B) Specific treatment of the pituitary, the thyroid and the sex glands : Stimulate each of the trigger areas shown in the adjoining diagram, through deep, alternating pressure for about a minute.

Repeat this treatment twice a day.

(C) Firmly clenching the teeth continuously for 2-3 minutes and then letting go helps to release physical tension.

16. REFLEXOLOGY FOR PREVENTING ILLNESS AND MAINTAINING PEAK HEALTH

It is said that, 'Prevention is better than cure'. We will say it is easier and cheaper too.

Given below are practical tips about preserving health through Reflexology.

Walk barefoot on uneven ground for atleast 5 minutes everyday. Alternatively, walk on dew-drenched grass early in the morning. These activities result into a stimulation of trigger areas for most bodily organs.

People who can't leave their homes, may derive the benefits of walking on uneven ground by making use of 'Reflexology Slippers/Insoles' or Wooden/plastic rollers, for 4-5 minutes each morning.

Other simple measures to influence all zones and, thereby, all organs include :

(1) Firmly clenching together the teeth continuously for 2-3 minutes once or twice every day or

(2) Firmly pressing the tips of fingers and the thumb of one hand against those of the other, for 2-3 minutes once or twice every day or

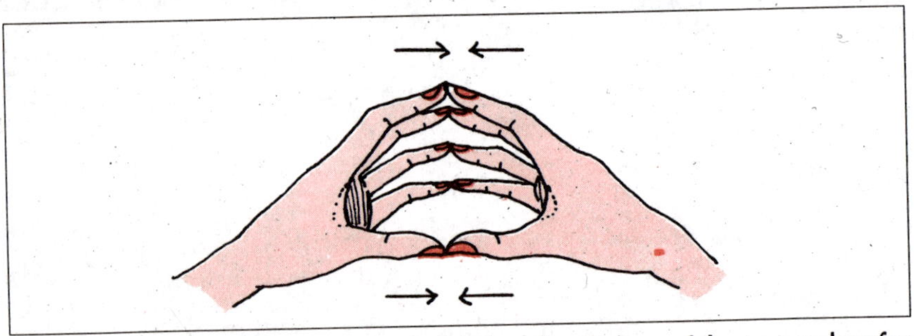

(3) Interlocking and pressing together the fingers of the two palms for 2-3 minutes once or twice every day.

APPENDIX

Suggestions for Therapists

We have presented in this chapter some practical suggestions and guidelines for the practising reflexologists, especially such budding reflexologists who have recently entered the field.

Many of the points mentioned here might be already known to you. However, we have presented them here with a view to reinforcing your knowledge. At the same time, we invite suggestions from you. They will help us to enrich our knowledge and to render future editions of this book more complete and useful for readers.

1. Try to acquire as much knowledge as possible. One source of knowledge are chapters 3 and 5 of this book. Read them once again to obtain guidance regarding method of pressure, duration of a treatment-session and frequency of treatments.

2. Fully explain to the patient what Reflexology is and what it strives to achieve. You may say, "Reflexology is a science of pressing specific spots on foot that have correspondence with internal organs and glands of the body. Working on these spots relaxes tension and helps the body to seek its own equilibrium".

3. Keep your nails well trimmed. You are aiming at helping your patient and not at injuring his skin with sharp, overgrown nails.

4. Make your patient either sit on a comfortable chair or lie down on a comfortable bed. The height of the chair/bed should be such that the patient's feet are at about your chest level after you sit down on a low table. This way you won't have to stretch your arms unduly or stoop forward while working on his feet. Prop his head up with a moderately thick pillow so that he can observe his feet being worked upon. Moreover, this helps you to keep an eye on his facial expressions and prevents you from inflicting unnecessary pain through excessive pressure. Though a certain amount of pain is inevitable, excess pain should be avoided because it tenses the patient.

5. Don't allow your patient to keep his hands interlocked during the treatment; ask him to keep his arms by his sides.

6. Before commencing with the treatment, make a careful examination of your patient's feet as regards temperature, skin thickness, state of circulation, corns, callouses, scars, etc.

7. Begin and end a treatment-session with any one of the many relaxation techniques described below :

Relaxation 1 :

Gently massage the dorsums and soles of the patient's feet, one by one, with your hands. Continue for about $\frac{1}{2}$ to 1 minute. This creates a pleasant sensation of warmth.

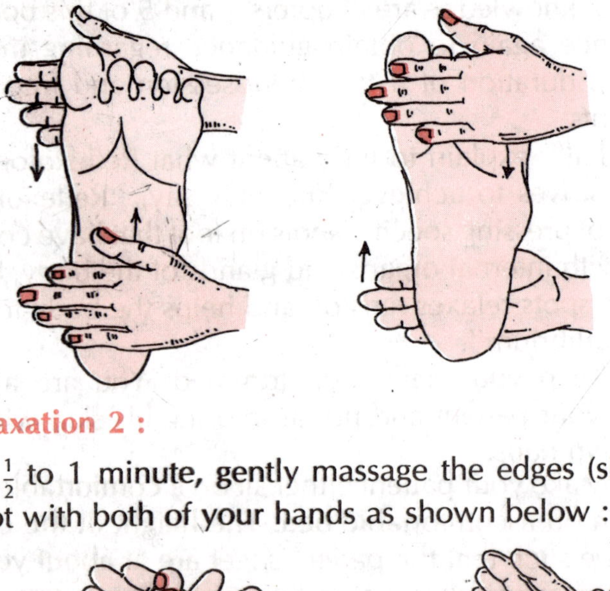

Relaxation 2 :

For $\frac{1}{2}$ to 1 minute, gently massage the edges (sides) of each foot with both of your hands as shown below :

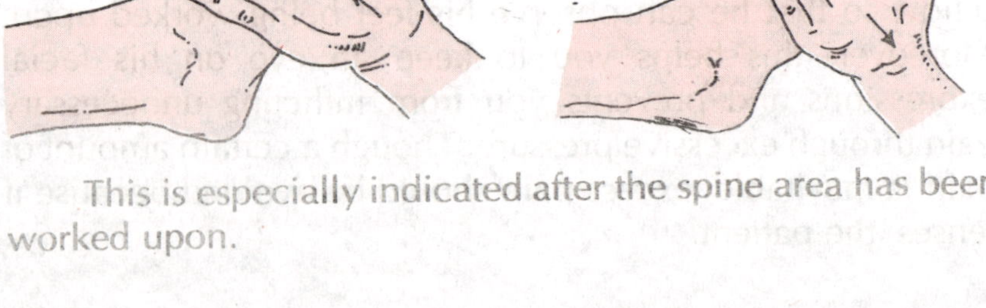

This is especially indicated after the spine area has been worked upon.

Relaxation 3 :

For $\frac{1}{2}$ to 1 minute, gently massage the sides of each ankle joint with both your hands as shown below :

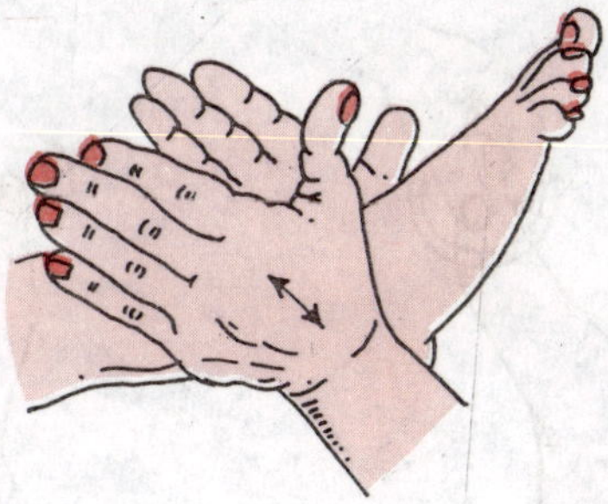

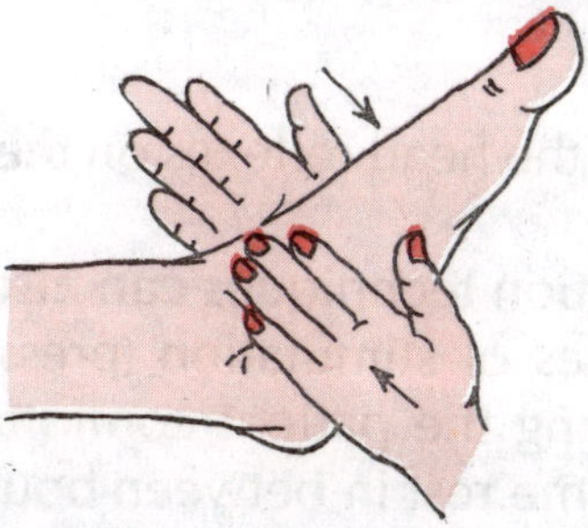

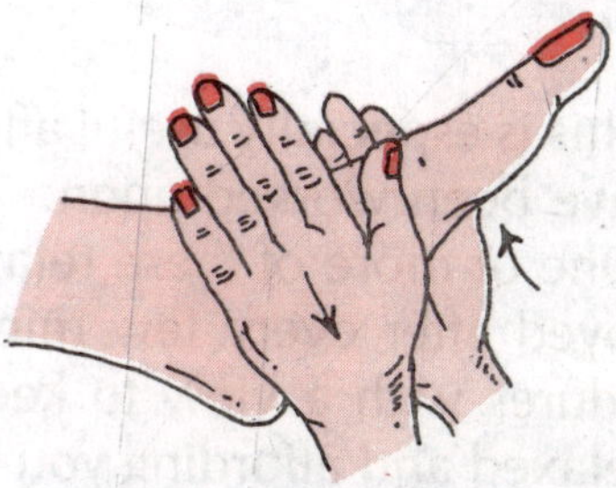

This is especially indicated after the pelvic areas have been worked upon.

Relaxation 4 :

For $\frac{1}{2}$ to 1 minute, gently rotate, clockwise as well as anti-clockwise, each ankle joint as shown below :

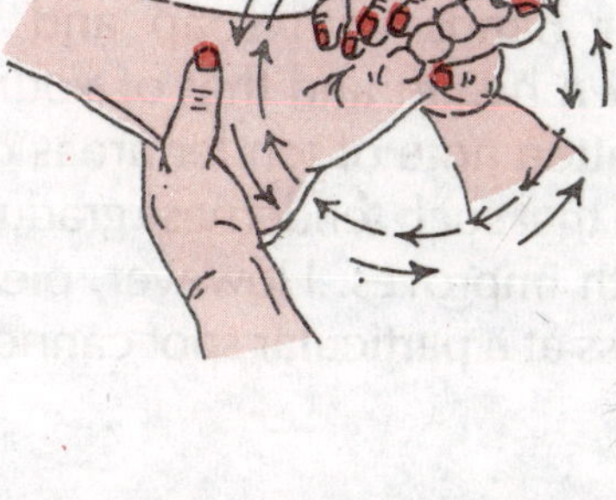

Relaxation 5 :

For $\frac{1}{2}$ to 1 minute gently rotate, clockwise as well as anti-clockwise) the big toe as shown below :

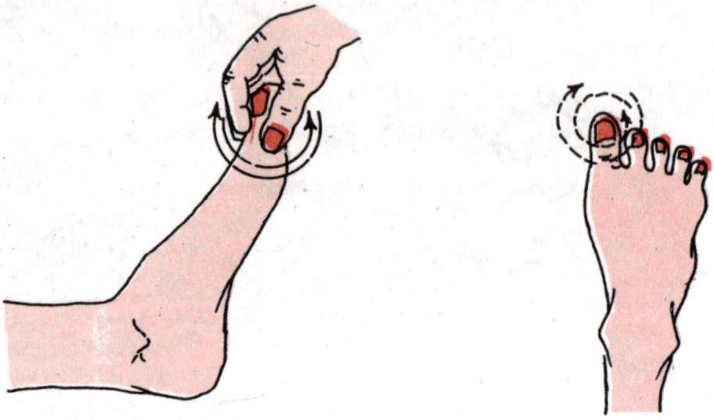

This is especially useful after the head reflexes on the big toe have been worked upon.

One or more of these relaxation techniques can also be employed after every few minutes of stimulation (pressure) procedures with a view to keeping the patient comfortable and relaxed and affording you some rest in between bouts of stimulation.

In other words, during a treatment-session relaxing procedures should be frequently alternated with (sandwiched between) stimulation procedures.

8. Do not work on corns, callouses, ulcerated/injured areas or varicosed veins. If these are obscuring some important reflexes, hands may be utilized so as to cover reflexes to all organs.

9. After the treatment is over, if possible, allow your patient to rest for 5-10 minutes. Meanwhile, for the sake of hygiene, wash your hands with soap and water. This is essential for your own health and that of your next patient.

10. Make a written note of tender areas detected. It is a common experience that such tenderness gradually diminishes as the patient's health improves. However, please understand clearly that tenderness at a particular spot cannot enable you to

diagnose a disease; this is just not possible because (a) in any particular part of the body, there is much overlapping of organs and (b) there are considerable variations in the locations (anatomy) of organs, from person to person. Again, tenderness is not necessarily a sign of an established disease. It may, just, be the result of a congestion or stress or functional overload in an organ. So don't volunteer to say : 'Since this spot is tender, that organ might be diseased.'

Remember : Diagnosing is the prerogative of a doctor. At best, tenderness at a particular spot on a foot may help a doctor to confirm the diagnosis he has made on the basis of clinical signs and symptoms. In other words, tenderness at some spot on the foot has to be correctly co-related with clinical findings (or investigational reports) before diagnosis can be arrived at.

Similarly, do not try to raise doubts about a doctor's diagnosis on the basis of tender spot/s you have found on the foot. Patient's complaints (symptoms), signs and reports of laboratory investigations are surer pointers to the presence (or absence) of a disease.

We reiterate : Never venture to diagnose. You may raise a false alarm or anxiety in the mind of your patient.

If your patient is too insistent to know about the significance of soreness of a particular spot on the foot, just say that it represents a particular region (e.g., head, neck, chest, abdomen, pelvis, spine, etc., as the case may be) of the body, where, perhaps, there is some congestion or malfunctioning. You should not say that the spot represents such and such organ.

If you previously were under the belief that in Reflexology you had found a great tool for diagnosis and that the statements made above are too harsh and discouraging, take heart in the fact that 'Reflexology works even without diagnosis'. Therein lies its strength and simplicity. Here, you have an edge even over a doctor! You can treat a case where doctors have been rendered helpless due to want of diagnosis ! !

11. Some patients, after three to six treatments, develop adverse reactions in the form of headaches, nausea-vomiting, cold, cough, mild fever, etc. Don't panic. These are, in fact, good signs indicating a cleansing process. Ask your patient to take rest and fast on water. The problems usually settle on their own in a day or two.

12. Avoid the temptation to prescribe anything, to anybody, at any time. It is illegal for any person who is not a registered medical practitioner to prescribe a medicine. This includes vitamins, mineral supplements, herbal medicines, tissue (Biochemic) salts and Homoeopathic medicines. No person expects to receive a prescription from a reflexologist. As a matter of fact, most persons usually seek Reflex Zone Therapy only after the various medicinal therapies have failed. If medicines could cure a person, he would never have come to you.

13. Do not guarantee results. It is just not possible to predict recovery because no two persons (even though suffering from the same disease) respond to Reflex Zone Therapy in the same way. Remember that forecasting is the prerogative of astrologers, not doctors. Not even a renowned surgeon guarantees success of the operation he is going to perform. Why then, should you, a much lesser mortal, promise success? Don't practise Reflexology indiscriminately. Be aware of its scope and limitations. It is irresponsible and unethical to raise false hopes.

14. If you are treating people other than your family members, be a thorough professional. Dress well; maintain a quiet and clean office; be punctual about time and see to it that your patients do the same. In this way, you will win the confidence of your patient and make him feel he is in safe, knowledgeable, competent hands.

Remember that the science of Reflexology is looking to you with great expectations. Don't let it down with unprofessional conduct. If you tarnish its image, good work of even ten Reflexologists may not be able to redeem it.

15. Do not accept to undertake the treatment of seriously

ill patients. Re-read chapter 1 for further guidelines. Patients with serious diseases need hospital-treatment. Reflexology is not an alternative to competent and urgent medical care.

16. Continue to learn; keep on reading to broaden and update your knowledge; be research-minded. Keep good records for statistical analysis in future. Remember, Reflexology is constantly changing and advancing. Everything about this science is not in this book nor any other book. The secret of success is continuing education, exploration and practice. It is said that 'Practice makes a man perfect'. However, we will say 'Perfect practice makes a man perfect'. If you walk southwards from Bombay, you can't reach Delhi, no matter how fast or how ceaselessly you walk. This book is intended to put you on the right path and in the right direction. We had to grope about in the dark for quite long and we learned by 'trial and error' method. But we wish that you be saved from such ordeals.

INDEX